REASON IN FAITH

REASON IN FAITH

On the Relevance of Christian Spirituality for Philosophy

ADRIAAN T. PEPERZAK

PAULIST PRESS
New York/Mahwah, N.J.

Cover design by Frank Vitale

Interior design by Millennium Wordpress

LIBRARY OF CONGRESS CATALOGING-IN-PUBLICATION DATA

Peperzak, Adriaan Theodoor, 1929–
    Reason in faith : on the relevance of Christian spirituality for philosophy / by Adriaan T. Peperzak.
        p.   cm.
    Includes bibliographical references.
    ISBN 0-8091-3857-3 (alk. paper)
    1. Philosophy and religion. 2. Christianity—Philosophy. I. Title.
BR100.P382 1999
261.5′1–dc21   98-53544
                                                                          CIP

Published by Paulist Press
997 Macarthur Boulevard
Mahwah, New Jersey 07430

www.paulistpress.com

Printed and bound in the
United States of America

Contents—

Reason in Faith

═══════════════

FOREWORD

Most of the chapters in this book originated as fragments of a lifelong engagement with questions about the meaning of being human. The wonder of our existence in the world—is there anything more surprising than that we *are?*—has amazed me from childhood. Usually it has delighted me, but I have also felt its burden; perhaps this prompted the awakening of philosophy's *éros* in me.

Within the intimacy of Franciscan friaries, I became acquainted with systematic philosophy and its history. This acquaintance began with lectures on Plato and Augustine (about whose "method" I wrote my first philosophical essay), Thomas and Bonaventure, Descartes, Spinoza, Kant and Hegel, Heidegger, Scheler, Sartre, and Marcel. This initiation resulted in an intertwining of spiritual contemplation and conceptual reflection, which I eagerly wanted to develop into a theology for our own time. During the fifties, in addition to my normal training in Roman Catholic theology, I devoured as much of the refreshing perspectives offered by Karl Rahner in the German world and by the adherents of the *Nouvelle Théologie* in France as I was able. Nevertheless, I arrived at the conviction that current dogmatic and moral theology ran so many centuries behind the dominant forms of ethos, art, science, and philosophy that the renewal sorely needed in theology would be possible only if we critically integrated what the great masters of modern and postmodern culture had already thought. This sparked my desire first to penetrate further into modern and contemporary philosophy. Later, I would confront the philosophical knowledge I had gathered with the rich traditions of premodern spirituality and theology in order to retrieve these in a way appropriate for the twentieth century.

On the basis of selected texts, professors in Leuven and Paris made me more familiar with the thought of Plato, Aristotle and Plotinus, Thomas, Kant, Hegel and Marx, Husserl, Heidegger, Merleau-Ponty, and Ricoeur. At the same time, the ideal of contemplation in the style of Augustine, Bonaventure, and Blondel remained intact. Most of these classics continued to accompany my studies, but others joined them: Anselm, Pascal, Spinoza and Leibniz, Fichte, Nietzsche, and Levinas have enriched me yet sometimes perplexed me as well. All these encounters have not changed my orientation, but they have broadened my perspective. The more I began to understand great thinkers, the more strongly I came to believe that Augustine's definition of *philosophia* as "faith seeking understanding" (*fides quaerens intellectum*) need not be reserved for an early-Christian or medieval way of thinking and being, but can be applied as a motto for all philosophers from Plato to Levinas. Many philosophers seem to have cut the ties between their life and their reflection, but in fact their prereflective engagements play an important role in the unfolding of their thoughts. No philosopher has ever given a completely rational justification for all of his starting-points and assumptions.

One of the most exciting aspects of historical reconstructions in which we attempt to retrieve what and how classical thinkers have thought consists in the discovery of the unproven, usually hidden, and often unreflected experiences from which their arguments and proofs take their departure. When such a reconstruction is fruitful, we achieve greater insight into the pluralism that characterizes Western philosophy. This pluralism does not exclude a certain affinity and agreement, however. One element that unites most (or even all) of the great philosophers is their search for meaning. No wonder: otherwise, why should thinking commence at all?

The quest for meaning is the core around which the discussions in this book revolve. It shows a preference for specific versions of belief and spirituality, and this preference is not always kept in the background. For readers who see themselves as "free spirits," it might be a reason to make light of the "theological" origin of the philosophy offered here. Does familiarity with chemistry, law, or mathematics offer a better point of entry for philosophy? Or is engagement in particular experiences of a profound but unscientific past a necessary condition for understanding anything about "meaning"? Perhaps "the search for meaning" is a shibboleth that calls us to some sort of solidarity. Does such a search express itself in the language of "a little flock," or in that of the media? Or of something in between, for example a discourse that picks up the thread of Plato and Augustine where Nietzsche and Heidegger left off?

In fact I want to show that "faith in search for understanding" can still be the motto for a twentieth-century hermeneutics of a life that is fascinated by the possibilities of thought. It is obvious that this brings me into conflict with some postulates of the philosophy that has dominated the last five hundred years, especially with the axiom that has functioned as an undoubtable dogma: philosophical thought is autonomous; it must and can unfold without any dependence on religion, faith or theology.

Since the beginning of the modern age, Christian theology has progressed in scholarliness but regressed in thinking. While, on the one hand, it has become very learned through exegetical and historical studies and very pastoral through its integration of insights from psychology, psychoanalysis, and sociology, on the other hand it has highlighted the experience of a faith not contaminated by religion, philosophy, or science. No one will argue that the bulk of contemporary theology has a good grasp of what is going on in philosophical thinking, nor that the bulk of philosophical discussions today demonstrate a familiarity with patristic, scholastic, modern, or contemporary theology. At the same time, belief in the power of reason has greatly diminished. Modern faith in the rigorous demonstrations of autonomous thought has been replaced by a revaluation of plausibility and rhetoric, opinions and customs, popular traditions and stories, authoritative texts and masters. Philosophy, too, has its authorities, traditions and celebrations, its esoteric jargons and sectarian exclusions.

And yet, many philosophers, even among Christians, believe that philosophy and theology must remain separate. On the level of explicit justification, they uphold the methodological "givens" that are the point of departure for modern thinking, especially the idea of human autonomy as separate from or even opposed to "supernatural" grace. Within the theoretical and normative framework of modern philosophy, the only choice was for autonomy; heteronomy was seen as a cause of "alienation." The fact that this choice has resulted in a mixture of atheism and agnosticism is one reason why reflective believers might feel urged to reconsider the relationship between believing and thinking.

Based on the conviction that the threefold separation between philosophy, theology, and spirituality is one of the causes of the contemporary hostility between a rather naive form of Christianity and the overreflective atheism of philosophy, this book offers a plea for the unbreakable unity of philosophy and theology. This unity must be further defined by a double self-critique, revealing both theological implications of the assumptions involved in philosophical methodology, and philosophical principles on which any serious theology rests. It cannot be authentic, however, unless it emerges from the lived experience of individual and collective histories in search of meaning—a meaning that holds the promise of some sort of wisdom.

Most chapters of this book originate in early versions written in Dutch and published in two small books, *Zoeken naar Zin* (Kampen: Kok Agora, 1990) and *Tussen Filosofie en Theologie* (Kampen: Kok Agora, 1991). In the thorough transformation of those versions into the English texts presented here, the following persons have assisted me: Aron Reppmann, whose translation into English was the basis for many changes in rhetoric and argumentation; Catriona Hanley, who carefully revised my English manuscript that has become chapter IX; Brian Chrzastek, who, through many suggestions, helped me in the last revision, and Scott Romans, who finalized the manuscript, correcting several remaining errors. Many others should be named if I were to credit all my oral and written sources—to begin with, my spouse, my parents, sisters and brothers, and all my other teachers, educators, and spiritual guides. In the awareness that I will never be able to redeem my debt to them and to the infinite source of their generosity, I can only express my deep and joyful gratitude.

Chicago–Wilmette, May 1998

I. PHILOSOPHY

There are many different conceptions of the nature and the tasks of philosophy. This makes it difficult for us to begin our discussion with a definition. To avoid this difficulty we could try to give a description instead—for example an historical or sociological description of persons, schools, texts or thoughts that are called philosophical in our time. For instance, we could start from the type of persons and skills that are required to teach philosophy in American universities. However, when we look closely at the various departments of philosophy, it becomes apparent that "philosophy" is a name for so many kinds of study that it is doubtful whether that name applies in each case to the same kind of undertaking. Between certain existential kinds of thinking, not easily distinguishable from experiential wisdom, and the mathematical precision of refined logicians, a great variety of philosophical styles has developed, each of which has its preferred questions and methods. In addition to the diversity of contemporary schools, philosophy is different from any science in that its history continues to play a primary role, especially

when it is practiced in the "Continental" style. The classical texts
of Plato, Aristotle, Augustine, Thomas, Kant, Hegel, Marx, Nietzsche, Wittgenstein, etc. remain somehow present. Even analytic,
positivistic, scientistic and empiricist schools continue traditions
whose foundations lie in past centuries. Some authors interpret
this fact as a symptom of decadence. According to them, the
"repetition" of outdated thoughts proves that Western philosophy is exhausted. Others see the plurality of existing philosophies as an argument for their own relativism. Still others defend
the idea that the "postmodern" period differs so radically from
all the preceding periods that we should even speak of a post-
philosophical era. However, any interpretation of the existing situation is itself a component of that situation. Each particular
diagnosis is linked to a particular philosophy, and this presents
one position among many in the wide field of "philosophy."

Can we escape this fragmentation by retreating to a margin
and developing from there a meta-philosophical theory about
the existing diversity of thinking and its history? This would presuppose that metaphilosophy can be practiced outside, above or
before philosophy. But is philosophy itself not precisely the kind
of thinking that looks at things from the highest, deepest, most
original and encompassing perspective? Is its purpose not to
ask—and, if possible, to answer—the most fundamental and ultimate questions? If so, it necessarily includes a discussion with
itself about its own situation and motivation, and all of its conditions and presuppositions.

A defensible interpretation of the contemporary situation runs
as follows. After Hegel's attempt to write a synthesis of twenty-
four centuries of thinking, philosophy has fallen apart into a disparate multitude of philosophies, most of which—despite their
deep-seated differences—radically critique the tradition and pro-
claim a new approach. They try to formulate a more radical perspective (or metaperspective) than the philosophies of the past
and to practice a more appropriate methodology. Most often
such an attempt is combined with a diagnosis and critique of
Western civilization and its history in the name of a better, more

radical, more realistic, more precise, or more enlightened future. However, none of these attempts have led to a generally accepted mode of philosophizing. The dispersion of philosophy into a plurality of partially or wholly exclusive styles still makes it impossible to declare, in the name of all its practitioners, what philosophy as such does, wants, knows, is or should accomplish. Each attempt to tackle these questions manifests the characteristic preferences of the person or school giving the answer.

Within philosophy the question of its proper nature and effects is one of the most difficult. The ability to answer it presupposes much more than familiarity with any existing philosophical practice. We must also know and explain in a reflective and metaphilosophical way what kinds of questioning, knowing, practicing, speaking, writing, etc. are constitutive for the various activities practiced by philosophers and how these activities ideally should be carried out.

The Greek word "philo-sophia" is often explained as a desire (*philia, philein*) for wisdom (*sophia*), an attachment to wisdom that is still underway and does not yet possess the desired wisdom. Initially, however, the verb *philein* meant, in this expression, something like "enjoy," "like," "love." *Philia* then also means friendship or love. "*Philosophia*" would therefore indicate the enthusiasm with which its practitioners participate in talking and writing about wisdom and in wise attitudes, behavior, tastes and judgments. If we understand the word in this way, it emphasizes that the main issue is not a concrete goal or specific treasure that can be conquered in a near or distant future, but rather is an ongoing occurrence, a rich and enjoyable practice which is nobody's property, though it invites whoever desires wisdom to join its discussions.

Philosophical wisdom, as it is approached by great thinkers past and present, is not a "gray theory";[1] it is the virtue that makes good manners in behavior and discernment possible. A human life is a failure if it is not sufficiently wise. The classics have conceptualized that wisdom in their skillful and, in a broad sense of the word, "technical" texts, thereby constituting a relatively independent discipline. Due to their theoretization, the intertwining of practical and contemplative elements, which is typical of wisdom, has become looser. Very early, definitory and argumentative aspects have been emphasized; dialogue and meditation were more and more replaced by learned treatises. Different functions were attributed to experience, observation, feeling, memory, imagination, thought, analysis, synthesis, demonstration, division, composition and systematization. The great thinkers have always maintained the bonds between theory and life, but the influence of the modern sciences has seduced many philosophers to see the "scientific" aspect of their own discipline as the core of their task and the main criterion for its work. For some schools, "scientific philosophy" has become synonymous with (genuine) philosophy as such. Whatever falls outside it they consider "literature" or mere sentiment. According to this scientistic conception, philosophy is distinguished from other sciences by its universal and fundamental character. Many topics that belonged to philosophy in the past have now been taken over by empirical sciences such as physics, psychology, sociology, linguistics, mathematics, etc. Because mathematics, physics and chemistry seem to produce the most exact, controllable, and efficient results, they are considered paradigms of cognitive achievement. From their perspective, all philosophy should conform itself, as much as possible, to their scientific standards. This demand imposes limits on the method and logic of philosophy: it can no longer do justice to all those phenomena that do not fit in the framework of the sciences. Among these phenomena morality, art, and religion, but also affectivity, sensibility, and science itself, are particularly interesting. Instead of wisdom, such a scientific philosophy produces insights whose scope is too narrow to be called "wise." To see these insights as exemplary for the truth implies a theoretical error: the scientific perspective is too incomplete to answer the question of which phenomena are genuine, worthwhile, basic, and so on.

Against the exclusion of wisdom from rigorous thought, a growing group of scholars demands that thinking be relevant for human existence as it is lived and experienced in its entirety and depths. The issue here is not beautiful visions or edifying narratives, but rather a thought that respects human life with its own questions by approaching it through a rigorous, but appropriate, logic. One of the tasks, for example, is to clarify the distinctions *and the intertwinings* between human life with its varieties of experience, and the dimensions of literature, science, common sense, and philosophy. Such tasks require distance *and* involvement in the issues that are at stake. By neglecting the bonds between philosophy and science, on the one hand, and literature, spirituality, faith, etc., on the other, philosophy falls to the level of a reflection that, however intelligent, is neither profound, nor, in the end, interesting.

If we emphasize the existential roots of philosophy, it is even more necessary to carefully distinguish philosophy from other, related but different, ways of involvement with actuality, truth and wisdom. What distinguishes it from myth and mythology, faith and theology, fascinating visions and healthy conceptions, poetry and literature, ideological doctrines and authoritarian dogmas? The modern answer to these questions arose from the conviction that philosophy is an autonomous kind of thought that begins with obvious and certain experiences and proceeds through logically coherent proofs. The autonomy of this thought was contrasted with the acceptance of authorities and opinions not supported by the same kinds of indubitable evidence or rigorous demonstration. Modern philosophy considers itself an emancipated, free thinking of individuals who defend universally valid theses and relations with regard to reality insofar as it is accessible to all normal people. However, the history of philosophy shows that not one of the philosophies that have been defended—including the most rigorously built systems—was entirely independent from unproven assumptions. Does this fact open the door to faith, authority and arbitrariness? No, philosophy remains the ongoing attempt to understand questions like the following: What is this? Why is it as it is? Why do we see and say and handle it thus? Should we see, handle, or approach it otherwise? Why does our saying and behavior have a history? To what extent is it possible to think without or with unproven assumptions, traditions, or authorities? The philosophical attempt is carried out through well-attuned experiences, very precise—if need be, even poetic—descriptions, and refined analyses. Its logic adapts to the modes in which the phenomena are given: as splendid or horrible, enjoyable or repulsive, trivial or overwhelming, important or uninspiring, and so on. Philosophy must not become less, but more exact and rigorous; however, more than in the past, it is aware of the multiplicity of possible perspectives and manners of unfolding; the ideal of a monolithic system can no longer be an assumption of its method.

To escape a self-destructive skepticism, without giving up the search for truth (even if "the truth" remains an ideal), philosophy must now try to understand why it has developed into an irreducible pluralism. Hegel's interpretation of historical philosophies as approximations of one overall synthesis has been exploded. Another, dialogical, interpretation has been proposed, but not yet sufficiently elaborated. Can we understand the history of philosophy as an ongoing discussion among independent thinkers, who, rooted in particular theories and practices, do not have to agree, but by their discussion establish the kind of kinship that belongs to friends of the truth? Such a discussion demands that the thinkers open their debate to life, logic, science, poetry and religion and concentrate on them in ways that are experienced, skillful and wise.

II. THE QUEST FOR MEANING

The quest for the meaning of (human) life is as old as thinking itself, but only since about 600 B.C. has it been done in a methodical and logical way, though it has not always relied on scientific theories. As intellectuals formed in the modern academy, however, we cannot entirely avoid the particular approaches taken by science, philosophy, and theology. Through our formation, we have integrated at least fragmentary pieces and popular versions of these approaches, and it would be very naïve to presume that we could free ourselves from all the assumptions that stem from our intellectual tradition.

In philosophy, systematic reflection about the meaning of life, society, speech, knowledge, good and evil, and so on was first practiced by the Greek teachers whom we call "sophists." Although we do not know them very well, we do know enough to typify them—somewhat anachronistically—as secularized and enlightened thinkers who no longer believed in the old myths, but instead attempted to practice and teach the art of argumentation, with an eye to political leadership. They were something

7

like those professors today who have given up the hope for truth
but concern themselves with private well-being and public success. Although there have been attempts in our time to restore
the honor of these intellectuals whom Socrates and Plato vili-
fied, Plato is the first genuine philosopher whom we can consult
in order to think well about being human in this world. He elevated the search for meaning to a level of reflection that is both
passionate and methodical, and in doing so he became the sire
of all thinkers who, not content with formal analyses, focus on
the indissoluble tie between living and thinking as the central
and all-determining issue for their considerations.

In several of his dialogues Plato argues that the philosopher,
just as a free person in general, should have "care for himself."[1]
This is a motivation that unites the philosopher with everyone
else. We find this "care" again, under the name *Sorge,* in one of
the most important books of the twentieth century, Martin Heidegger's *Being and Time.* It is clear, however, that the concept has
undergone several transformations in the meantime. To name
an important difference between Plato and Heidegger: the first
translates "care for oneself" directly into "care of the person for
his own soul" *(psychē).*[2] Although the meaning of *psychē* for Plato
and his "dualism" must be more carefully reconstructed than it
usually is, it remains true that his concentration on the *psychē*
over against the *sōma* has been a decisive source of Western
spiritualism, with all the theoretical, practical, and affective per-
plexities that belong to it. In contrast, Heidegger (along with
Nietzsche) is a harbinger of our attempts to respect the "wisdom
of the body" and to restore the unity of the person—a difficult
task, which we have not yet accomplished.

For the moment, however, instead of dwelling on the differences, I want to emphasize that the history of philosophy can be
read as one long reflection on one constellation of questions
which can be formulated thus: What does it mean that persons are
concerned about (the meaning of) their own lives? How can they
best achieve this? Why is one way of being concerned better than
another? In the Western tradition, this reflection has taken the

form of an attempt to discover *the truth* and *the good* of reality. However, the terms "true" and "good" have been closely associated with the knowing intellect and the acting will, and many thinkers have neglected or even repressed the truth of the affective life; moreover, the meaning of "true" and "good" has exploded into a multitude of interpretations. Therefore, it seems better to begin with a much vaguer, but less compromised and perhaps more originary word: "meaning." Starting from this beginning, I will defend the following thesis: the radical and authentic significance of philosophical thinking consists in a thoughtful quest for meaning.[3] The importance of this thesis lies especially in the indissoluble bond it maintains between the logical, epistemological, and metalogical rigor of thinking that must be learned as a skill, and a life lived as a passionate pursuit of meaning.

But what is (the meaning of) "meaning"? Do we not already violate responsible thinking when we use such vague terms as "the quest for meaning," "the meaning of life," "lived life," and so on? Must we not begin with definitions of "meaning," "life," "searching," "questioning," etc., if we do not want to lose ourselves in a tangle of words that says little or nothing because it lacks delineations and distinctions? If this demand is valid, it requires us also to establish what a definition means and how it is constituted, in what contexts it is possible or impossible, and when it is not only possible but also advisable or necessary. Anyone who considers such questions quickly discovers that it is not always possible or beneficial to define an issue or an experience, especially at the *beginning* of a fundamental reflection. To demand at the beginning of an argument or dialogue that the speakers define what they are talking about is to begin from epistemological assumptions that must first be justified themselves. If these assumptions are not immediately justified, then such a demand does not reveal a reflective insight, but rather a cheap and quasi-philosophical naïveté. The presupposition that everything can be defined, for example, implies wrongly that everything we can name can be delineated or delimited. If this were the case, many things, aspects, and experiences would be excluded from our speech, beginning with everything that is unlimited or infinite. What is the justification for such an exclusion? Moreover, such a commitment to definitions accepts that everything that is delimited can be characterized *stante pede* according to its essential moment, but does this not precisely require an adequate and comprehensive analysis of the issue that we want to define? If that is so, a definition seems more appropriate at the end of an argument, as a summary of the findings, than at the beginning. As Spinoza and Hegel have demonstrated, an issue that is to be defined, particularly if it is a central or basic issue, cannot be isolated from other issues to which it is essentially connected. Such connections also must be defined in order properly to delineate the main point. Proceeding in this way, Hegel came to the conclusion that the truth of any single issue implies the truth of all others and their coherence in the whole: the truth is in the whole *(die Wahrheit ist im Ganzen)* and the truth is the whole *(die Wahrheit ist das Ganze)*. It is not my concern here whether this conclusion (along with its assumptions) is true. For the moment it is enough to see that definitions do not possess the priority that is often claimed for them.

Let us return to "meaning." However vague and indeterminate this word may be, many recognize it as indicating an all-important, essential, and indispensable element, without which a human life cannot be good or even fully be lived. There is something in us to which the word "meaning" appeals. We feel addressed and touched, affected by it. Apparently there is a sort of affinity and familiarity with meaning, to which we can appeal even before we have attempted to say anything precise about it. Moreover, that already-present familiarity with meaning functions as a criterion when we set to work at clarifying what we mean by it.

The prominence of the word "meaning" in a number of the most important texts of our time has nothing to do with an aversion to clarity or distinctness. Rather, the use of this word, even without our being able to define it precisely, is a sign of our sensitivity toward what is "really real" (and which loves to conceal itself), and also of a certain fear of disfiguring or chasing away what ultimately is at stake. True, there is the danger of a paralyzing laziness when the question "what is the meaning of all of this?" arises. But to fight against this temptation we must be cautious enough to safeguard a real or possible meaning by not forcing it into a ready-made pattern. Applying such patterns is even more violent if the issue is in itself obscure or mysterious than when they are imposed upon self-evident or transparent phenomena.

As with such words as "mystery" and "God," we cannot rid the word "meaning" of its indeterminacy, certainly not immediately and perhaps never. *First,* it does not indicate any particular thing: "meaning" is nothing like an object, a substance, a person, an angel, a god, a world, a totality, a spirit, or an entity. It is more like "something by means of which" things, persons, gods, the universe, and even God are "worthwhile," "meaningful." A *second* aspect of meaning is that it corresponds to a deep but hidden impulse, an original pathos and a desire that drives us. In some moments or periods of our lives, we are forced into the awareness that life ultimately is not worth living if we do not feel in some way or another that it is "meaningful." For some people this awareness is constant, and when they philosophize, it is evident in their way of thinking. A *third* attribute of "meaning" is that it is essentially obscure and hidden. It cannot be grasped or seen, but only sensed or felt. When it is represented in the form of an image, a concept, or a judgment, we should be suspicious of its appearance: "This is too superficial to be 'meaning' itself"; "I will not let myself be taken in by this." Precisely in its hiddenness and obscurity, meaning is experienced as what is the most "real," "actual," and active. It holds life in tension as that which, in the end (and from the beginning), is at stake—as "the real (no)thing."

The characterization of "meaning" just given has made a transition from "meaning" in a very indeterminate and general sense of the word to that of the *ultimate* meaning of human life. From this point on, I will indicate the latter sense by capitalizing "Meaning."

Perhaps, then, we can summarize the aspects just enumerated by saying that Meaning is neither a thing nor a puzzle, but rather a secret, or even a mystery. A way of thinking that appropriately answers to this, a "heart" that "(cor)responds" to Meaning, has a "feel" or a "sense" for it, but Meaning remains mysterious. Such a way of thinking is both rigorous—and thus genuine—and interwoven with an experience that it attempts to clarify by testing it for genuineness and depth. Thus this thinking takes on the character of a quest, an adventure, an experiment.

What we have said so far is only a beginning. Since "Meaning" is concealed in the depth of a mystery, thinking about it is possible only by circling around it, cautiously approaching the mystery by reflecting its radiance. In this way, thinking about Meaning proceeds by being concerned for many other things—questions, desires, aspirations, phenomena, resistances, and oppositions—that refer to Meaning. It is not an object that we can set up in front of ourselves in order to encircle it so as to possess it. Rather, it is a "something" (but not a thing) that is continually present in a specific, "mysterious," but real, relationship with all other "things" (animals, persons, nature and culture, history and eternity) when we are engaged with them—for example, when we concentrate on them in our thinking. Drawing near to Meaning, then, consists of tracing a network of references; this succeeds or fails according to how we bring the world of persons and things into speech. The "tone" and "style" of such an approach, the voice in which it is spoken, its earnestness that is not without irony, its careful and level-headed elation, a certain form of grateful patience, etc., reveal to us whether or not someone maintains a bond with meaning. Meaning's secrecy requires that our speech about it be indirect; a direct access seems not to be available in language.

Human Existence as a Quest for Meaning

Living in search of Meaning is a specific way of experiencing time. Can we clarify this experience?

What and how is the time in which a human life is played out? If we reflect a little bit though not very deeply about this question, we encounter the time-concept of classical natural science. According to this concept, time is a series of homogeneous points that, in their succession, form a continuous line in which we can distinguish changes and occurrences. This gives us the idea of a linear succession of homogeneous moments without beginning or end. In addition to this image, many people accept as self-evident that earlier events influence what comes after them, while the reverse is not the case. Against this conviction, the Aristotelian conception of time (still resonating with some of our own experiences) asserts that nature and culture are full of unrealized purposes, which, operating out of a possible future, have an effect in the present and even in the past. Justification for this teleological interpretation is found in such phenomena as a melody (in which the first tones will have received their own significance and proper sound only when the melody is finished), the growth of a tree, or the growing-up of a child. While this teleological interpretation contradicts the idea that, although earlier events have an impact on later ones, the reverse is not true, it can still be compatible with the conception that time is a succession of homogeneous and equal portions.

The time of human life, however, cannot be experienced as a series of equal moments indifferent to each other. It is evident from the distinctly human way of "having time" or "being temporal" that human existence is not an object of physics and that natural science cannot tell us much about its existential temporality. These statements have nothing to do with the well-known contrast between objective and subjective knowledge. The *specific* manner of observing, combining, calculating, and reasoning of modern natural science is just as subjective as the perspectives of Aristotle or Bergson; but every perspective offers a chance to discover what belongs to the objects in view and is in this sense "objective," even if it allows for a narrow perception only.

How is time manifested to someone who has given up the illusion of being able to objectify it "from the outside" because he or she respects the encompassing temporality of all experiencing and objectifying thought? With regard to this difficult question,

I can only give a few hints for an answer here. To begin with, we can state that the life of every person is a passage from birth to death. This shows that the time of life is delimited, that there are boundaries to everyone's human existence. The limits themselves, however, cannot be grasped; they are not given empirically to those who try to speak about their own mortality.

Death

When we speak about "death," we easily hypostasize an occurrence that 1) is not a thing or a substance, and 2) radically differs from all other possibilities that occur in time. The hypostatic character of such an approach is obvious if we represent death in the image of the Fates or of the Grim Reaper with his scythe. Death then becomes an enemy who overpowers us, and this expresses an aspect of our anxiety. At the same time, however, we realize all too well that this anxiety is directed not at these fanciful images, but precisely at "the nothing" into which we threaten to disappear.

Dying or perishing is always ambiguous. On the one hand, it is a process of *still* living, but doing so in a dwindling and nearly hopeless way; thus the perspective of the future is maintained, although, like the sand in an hourglass, it becomes ever more narrow until it finally disappears. On the other hand, death is the actual falling into the condition of no longer being the human being I was up to that point. We know this condition from the outside by observing the corpses of others. A corpse is certainly very different from a living body and a "dead person" is a contradiction in terms. Every corpse presents us with a riddle: "what does this have to do with my being dead someday, which makes me anxious now?" I cannot gather any experience of my own being-dead, and thus I cannot have a genuine concept of it. When we euphemistically define dying as "leaving the world," this suggests too strongly that our existence continues beyond this separation, although we have no actual experience of this. So long as I have not died, I do not know what being-dead is (what sort of "being" is this?), but when I have died, I am no more. Thus I cannot contend now that I will know or experience anything at all then.

However, we do know *that* we will die, and this certainty is definitive both for the meaning of our life and for the time within which this life unfolds. The knowledge of our mortality is not an abstract consciousness; I experience it, concretely and from within, through the threatening approach of my own death. Mortality is an essential moment of the presence in which we live; it permeates all our feeling and perceiving. If we are realistic, we make no plans for eternity. However, it is not easy to abide by this limitation, and hence we succumb to many illusions about tomorrow, next year, or later. Our mortality seizes us in experiences of fatigue, sickness, injury, exhaustion, and aging. The many ways we eagerly stifle our apprehension of death show how well we understand that the transition from the last remainder of life to death is not a part of any history; it is not a genuine event— we cannot "place" death—in any experiencable moment since it is primarily the having-become-impossible of all events. Since it excludes every possibility that something may happen, death does not fit within the framework of the world or the time of our life. It remains alien, though singularly definitive. How could we possibly welcome it? The impossibility to which everything leads, the relentless finitude of all humanity, the mute but certain (and yet always too early and unexpected) fact that the thread of life will be torn away, color all our activities, and, more fundamentally, all the moods in which we find ourselves. Everything leads to nothing; the truth of this can assault us when we chip a tooth or when youth lies irretrievably behind us.

Birth

How do we know, apart from what others tell us, about our own birth? We have gone through it, but we do not remember anything about it. Is our knowledge of it only a second-hand knowledge or a conclusion on the basis of an induction? If that were the case, we would not have a single experience of our own entry into the world. The indiscoverable beginning of my life-history would be hidden behind experiences in which I have discovered that I already exist. Only by a backward projection of recollections could I "construct" for myself a first moment of being-in-the-world.

As with death, I also experience "shadows" of my birth. My first appearance is suggested in many (re)birth-like events of my life. There is something astonishing about some new occurrences, as if everything first began with them. Waking up, feeling renewed after an illness, smelling the fragrances of the coming spring, seeing the dawning light of a new day are experiences in which existence has something of "the first time": a sort of (re)creation in which life becomes new.

However, in all of these occurrences there is also the more or less concealed experience of always already having been on the way. I experience myself as having become what I am now and was before; I am and will be myself thanks to the givens and past events of family, culture, life, and nature, which have shaped what I am now and continue to shape what I still hope to become. I have emerged from a past that I have neither made nor chosen. As heir to an inheritance that preceded me, I realize that human existence consists not in the free projection of a world, but rather in the integration of a history that took on its own form and dynamics long ago, before I appeared. A part of that heritage has become the flesh and blood that is I, while I have left aside or put to use other possibilities that have been given to me. I participate in a past that is much older than I; however much originality may characterize my participation, it has been possible only on the basis of a radical receptivity. Just as death indicates to me that I am at the mercy of an absolute impossibility, so I recall my own birth to the extent that I experience my life as a limited and personalized but nevertheless inexhaustible possibility that comes over me, and which I can never fully explain.

Having been born is a direct refutation of the myth of human autarky. The beginning of my existence with all its subsequent wealth and works lies in an absolute receptivity. My own activity can only be a response to this beginning, either by acquiescing to it or by seeking to destroy it. Positive and meaningful actions are possible only as the realization of a fundamental possibility that opens other possibilities, a possibility that is simply given without question. The catchword "self-actualization" is ambiguous: a human life is not the autonomous execution of a self-instituted plan, but the (free and responsible) *self-experiencing* of what befalls me or happens to me whether or not I willed it or deserve it.

If receptivity and "bornness" characterize human existence, we should not be eager to see an active "giving of meaning" as the ultimate key or principle.[4] On specific levels of life and in specific circumstances meaning can be generated or given by human initiatives, but *Sinngebung* suggests too much autarky. Meaning is not a product; it is experienced primarily as an invitation or a summons, a suggestion or an urging that calls us. It cannot be made or conquered. All products and possessions are, in the end, disappointing. Whatever I make or possess always says to me: "This is not (yet) what we seek."

To live my life is to participate in my having been born and brought up within it. My life, as an individual, and in this sense original, realization of the suggestions that have come to me, concretizes some particular possibilities of human existence within a culturally and socially determined context. Such suggestions are experienced as a destiny and a task or obligation. At the same time, however, it stands firm that fulfilling this destiny leads to the nothingness of death.

Time and Meaning

"Meaning" cannot be known as a thing, a fact, or an event. Some texts, particularly mystical ones, describe moments in which someone is overpowered by a peak experience of "light" or "union," but even though the authors of these texts may perhaps have discovered or recognized "Meaning" itself, such descriptions are not sufficient to convey the meaning of everyone's life.

"Ordinary" time, too, the everyday conduct of life, needs to be meaningful. Each individual's life is a search motivated by a basic desire for the secret of its ultimate meaning.

Searching for meaning requires attention and concentration. With the help of familiar traditions of spirituality, we learn receptivity and experiment with forms of attunement. The Meaning cannot be produced or acquired by striving or working alone; its transcendence is evident when we discover that it is rather a gift that surpasses all works and conquests. Its realization demands not only ascesis but also acceptance. The self-discipline it demands must, therefore, be oriented just as much toward cultivating an appropriate receptivity.

Openness for meaning avoids inauthenticity. Pseudo-meaning includes all sorts of fake splendors and delights: not only dependence on drugs, sex, or money, but also infatuation with science, morality, and religion, when these are cherished as substitutes for the search for absolute meaning itself. The art of becoming free for Meaning consists in getting loose of all our loves, *without* despising anything of what is indeed loveable. Infatuation threatens the possibility of a healthy distance; a turning is needed to keep us oriented toward Meaning itself. Fascination, especially with noble endeavors, is tempting, but to identify Meaning with a supposedly known entity, even with religion or the "God" of public beliefs, makes transcendence disappear. This is idolatry, and it creates the deepest dissatisfaction, as is manifest, for example, in the melancholy aura of every kind of addiction or fanaticism. Enthusiasm finds it difficult to remain within the limits of the dimension inhabited by its god(s). On the other hand, though, do we not fall into another form of idolatry if we decide to abide by those limits? Is such heroism the fruit of self-contempt engendered by pride?

It is probably inherent in the nature of Meaning that turning from the finite to the ultimate must be something that happens to us as a sort of birth. Someone I respect speaks seriously to me or leads me into confusion, say, by articulating the contradictions of life (or by letting me express them myself). Or someone who is

dear to me suddenly dies. Such events can bring me to "reflection," to a "turning" or "conversion." Of course, I can also flee
from the confrontation or deflect it. However, a more promising
approach to Meaning assumes that, at least "deep down," I am
moved by a passion for it that lets itself not be discouraged. Such
a passion unites within itself the passivity of a fundamental
receptivity and the dynamism that vows "victory or death"—a
passion, thus, that "conspires" with Meaning itself in that it spurs
me to seek what I cannot possess.

The Path of Life

Human life can be seen as a pathway. In the absence of clear
markings, it must be discovered and cleared through the ongoing
process of life itself. Must we represent Meaning as an endpoint
toward which the path of life should lead, or can it realize itself in
the very stance and steps of life itself?

A Roman Catholic catechism that was still being used in the
thirties answered the question "For what purpose are we on the
earth?" with the statement: "We are on the earth in order to serve
God and thereby to go to heaven." This answer could also be formulated in other ways, such as: "Human life, which is a passage
from birth to death, is a process that derives its meaning from
preparing for a goal, which (if life is successful) is realized only at
the end of that process." Or even: "Through living a good life, a
person achieves (or earns) the salvation that begins when his or
her life ends; but until death—as long as we are alive—we must
endure much deprivation, including many forms of apparent
meaninglessness that emerge during life." According to such
answers, the full meaning of life does not lie within life itself, but
only after it has ended. But what could "after" mean here? Does
life itself have no ultimate meaning at all? In this perspective,
what gives meaning to life would lie outside of it and yet be what is
most sought within life. This mortal existence would be a preliminary existence and a precursory practice, not "the real thing."
Life would still be a serious concern, insofar as it is a condition of

another, more genuine existence, but how could we say anything about this more genuine existence, since death separates us from the present circumstances to which our understanding is limited?

Another way to question the teleological orientation presented above is to inquire into the meaning of decline and old age. If it is true that the meaning of life is to be found not in, but after, this life, what kind of meaning and how much of it can we expect in the midst of a slow process of dying and decay? Does becoming old truly make us grow in wisdom and compassion? Is it not equally probable that we might rather regress, even psychologically and spiritually? Particularly in times of transition, most elderly people seem neither well-adapted to the changes nor able to orient younger generations through wise instruction. Is the purpose of old age to learn more acceptance by giving in to the frailty of mind and body? But is not such an acceptance itself already a sign of growing meaninglessness? Or is it rather a partial realization of the ultimate meaning?

If in all the stages of life everything is staked on a hereafter, then the entire significance of each stage relies on how it contributes to the actualization of the last one, but this, being no longer a stage of life, is only realized after death. If such were the case, the meaning of a human life would lie in a continual preparation—purification, practice in virtue and openness, etc.—culminating in the realization of "Meaning." But is it conceivable for there to be an intrinsic link between the purity of perfect acceptance and the termination of life, which then would be the condition of obtaining the desired end? Why could a long-living person not already have attained in his youth the highest purity of spirit that is possible for this person? What is the meaning of such a life's continuation?

Fixing our attention on the afterlife continually defers life itself ("some day I will live meaningfully"). Can we experience the whole of life as not yet meaningful, and therefore as an always unfulfilled wandering? Endless postponement denies the possibility of a full meaning appropriate to each of the different phases of life, even though it may be replaced by other stages.

The meaning of various phases cannot be reduced altogether to their being instrumental in preparing for later periods, nor as moments whose entire meaning is integrated into the next one. Childhood, adolescence, adulthood, and old age all have their own irreducible possibilities and suggestions for meaning. Many elements of a child's life, for example, are taken along and integrated in a person's growing-up, but much of its meaning is irretrievably lost; only children can realize it. Hence nostalgia for an earlier time is not always a sign of weakness.

In the philosophical literature, there is particularly little to be found about the true nature and meaning of the different phases of life. If what we have just said is true, however, it is an important task for philosophers (in collaboration with developmental psychologists) to understand those phases as specific possibilities of meaning. If every phase is relatively independent, each transition from one to the next has an element of death and rebirth. Thus, going through such a transition is one of the ways we experience the shadows of birth and death. By losing essential possibilities, we get a sense of the gravity of death; in our labor-pains, we receive new possibilities and discover the significance of (re)birth. Such a transition is like death insofar as we cannot transport ourselves back into the ways of feeling, seeing, and thinking that were ours at an earlier stage, for example as children. We can no longer be what we once were; even memory can no longer reconstruct the true character of our own past. But if the transition—at the price of some sort of dying—is successful, we experience the joy of renewal.

Nonetheless, the view that postpones the meaning of life to the moment of its end does indicate an important experience. A life is one whole, and in spite of the great differences between its periods, it forms a "figure of time" that appears as a whole not only to outsiders who outlive it, but also to my self-experience when I survey my own life. Self-reflection implies calling up my own past and anticipating the remainder of my life in a global way while asking: how does this life of mine fit together? How has it gone, and how might it go from here on? What was, what is, what will be its meaning?

The meaning of a life is never finished; until we die, it is still uncertain whether we will have lived a meaningful life, for everything can still go wrong. Hence the famous question of Solon, on which Aristotle meditated in the first book of his *Ethics:* can we be called happy before we die?[5]

It is difficult for us to think about the whole of a human life in any other terms than those of a final purpose: what is realized or achieved in it? For example, what was the purpose of Socrates' existence? Yet something about this question sounds strange. "Destiny" fits better here: "What was Socrates' destiny?" "What is my destiny?"

When we see a human life as purposive, we think of its possibilities as "coming to bloom." A person, like a full-grown, blooming tree, can enjoy a prosperous period that seems to display the best possibilities of human existence in full splendor. This does not apply to every life, since many obstacles and handicaps can prevent a blooming maturity, but some successful exemplars can give us an idea of what "fully human" might mean. Must we now say that the meaning of human existence is shown in good, successful maturity, and thus evaluate the preliminary stages of life as mere anticipation and old age as decay? But when exactly is one fully grown, and what is the standard for the full actualization of exemplary human possibilities?

Peak times vary, depending on which possibilities are to be actualized. The fruitful time of life is very different for a runner, a poet, a physicist, a philosopher, and a mother. However, we are not considering the exemplary realization of a *specific* activity, but rather the essential flowering of human life as such. Although these two questions are not entirely separable, neither are they identical. To avoid being misled by them, we must reflect on the assumption from which they proceed, namely, that life has a purpose, and that this is to be sought in some kind of flowering.

Does a plant or a tree have a purpose? If so, is that purpose expressed in its flowering? We enjoy the blossoms of a cherry tree, but do we appreciate them more than its fruits, which require the death of the blossoms? If we like the fruits, does this include that the flowering tree has lost its appeal for us? A person is not a tree; moreover it is difficult to separate the purpose of a plant from the values that humans attach to it, while a human life and the person who values it share the same reality. Is the true meaning of a human life realized in blooming or in bearing fruit, in the glorious but fleeting exhibition of beauty, or in the production of enduring works that bring some measure of victory over mortality?

Good, successful products such as a beautiful text, an impressive statue, or an excellent law do not necessarily make their authors meaningful persons, although there is at least something good and meaningful in this kind of self-actualization. Even leaving behind well-educated children is no proof of a fulfilled existence. In the last example, the educator must already know when a person is good; the idea of a "product" presupposes here an answer to the question of Meaning. Such a question cannot be solved by reproduction or by passing the question on.

A Suggestion

A human life realizes meaning, albeit in a deficient form, by following the guidance of its essential transcendence: its inborn desire and search for Meaning. Accepting the facts and possibilities of being human here and now, life is more than preparation for a distant meaning; it is a realization of Meaning itself. Whoever thus pursues the question as it attracts and inspires the here-and-now demonstrates the possibility that Meaning can be lived even while it is still hidden. The awareness of this possibility is expressed in grateful remembrance, hopeful courage, and reconciled acceptance concerning one's engagement with the joys and griefs of the earth. If familiarity with the present unites gratitude and hope as modes of human (e)motion, temporality is experienced as the way in which Meaning discloses itself (however elusively) and demands to be enacted. This disposition makes it

possible for us to agree with existence as it is. Evil and grief are
then accepted as belonging to the enigma of existence; although
they cannot be understood, neither can they destroy the splendor of the universe, though they may obscure and damage it.

A peaceful mood gives birth to a mixture of seriousness, joy,
and irony that is able to endure the ravages inflicted on the
world by nonsense and evil. The "soul's concern for itself" is a
devotion to what is most real, in the awareness that its brilliance
and its obscurity are inseparable.

If what we have said here is true (or nearly true), we must
maintain that Meaning can always be experienced in every step
of the walk of life, even though that experience will usually occur
in a fragmentary way, mixed with half-sense or nonsense. Meaning "wants" to be lived here-and-now. Now is the *kairos*. Everything is full of mystery. All births and all declines are both
enigmatic and significant. Meaning is not neatly rounded off nor
is it a "happy ending"; it is always possible in the here-and-now
that is both born and dying, rich in new opportunities and frag-
mented by decay. In this never-ending story, Meaning is present
as the principle of motion and emotion, but also of rest and
patience. At the same time it holds itself at a distance, since its
realizations here and now are usually deficient and only partial.
All nonsense is an aping of meaning. The devil is God's ape.

The most striking deficiency in the realization of Meaning,
which traditionally has also received the most emphasis, is evident in the experience that my life could have been better: I did
not achieve my goal, because I lacked the ability, the generosity,
or the daring; I have not yielded to the exacting discipline of concentration or to the tedious monotony of training. Another lack
of meaning arises in various forms of pseudo-meaning: TV,
rhetoric, power, greed, sex, and science tend to enslave us; if they
rule, they make us loathe ourselves, but we are quite clever at
avoiding the warnings conveyed to us by this loathing. A third
way in which Meaning escapes us is evident in experiences that
tell us: "This is not (yet) it. This is not the text I wanted to write,
the life I wanted to live, the love I sought." Even if I do not have a

clear image of how my text or my love or I myself should be, I can still say with certainty: my life (or text or love) is not (yet) such as it should be. The perfect meaning that should be actualized is perhaps operative, but in a deficient mode.

"I am not yet where (and what) I should be." Will I ever coincide with "the purpose," with my destiny? It is a painful experience to live with a mixture of meaning and lack of meaning; in the midst of this suffering, I hope for a future in which there is a better chance for the Meaning for which I exist. This horizon holds me in tension, leading from deferral to deferral and from anticipation to anticipation. Thus the idea can arise that I will be fine *"later"*–when I am grown up, capable, old and wise, good and level-headed–"some time" in an indeterminate future. Thus the perfect Meaning is continually present *and* delayed. Will I pass up all the here-and-nows until finally I am dead? But then I will never have met with what seems to be the most and only important thing. Desire for the perfect fulfillment that should and might be realized in the future does not destroy the present– be it incomplete–reality of Meaning. "Rhodos is here; here is the place to leap and dance."[6] Today is the day of the secret. The Good is nearby.

III. The Quality of Life

I.

Many questions are involved in discussions about "the quality of life." What do we mean by the word "quality" when we use it to qualify the whole of our life? Why do we use the term "life" in this context, rather than "human being," "existence," or "spirit"? Why does asking about the quality of life cause such seriousness, difficulty, and sometimes even despair in us? How can we best tackle this question? What method must we follow in meditating on it?

These questions follow the typically over-reflective tendency of philosophy today. Before we deal with any of them, we are tempted to devote ample time to defining the problem, determining the methodological requirements for a possible answer, and critically evaluating previous approaches. Such metatheoretical considerations can captivate us for so long that we have no time or energy left for dealing with the questions themselves. It is entirely possible that the research program runs out of time or breath even before we finish the preliminary considerations.

The current penchant for metatheoretical reflection is a direct result of the modern conception of philosophy, expressed in the works of Bacon, Hobbes, Descartes, Leibniz, Kant, and many others. In their attempt to emancipate themselves from all authorities and conflicting traditions, they tried not only to establish a foundation of truth that everyone in principle could check, but also to codify universally valid rules that would guarantee the discovery of solid and certain truths. The question of a universal method for all investigations became a major issue, and many thought that philosophy should begin with a critical account of the logical and epistemological presuppositions that must rule the study of its topics. Although many successful scholars do not allow themselves to be distracted from their creative work by endless reflections on methodological hypotheses and practices, it is a pretty general requirement that all categories and rules must be justified before they may be trusted.

The modern ideal of a foundational metatheory is governed by the wish to assume a neutral standpoint with regard to all doubts and divergences concerning basic issues such that one could see and comprehend reality in an "objective" and universally valid way. For a long time, thinkers have wanted to analyze and rationally reconstruct the universe so that we could understand it as a transparent system. Apart from the technical applications such knowledge would provide, it would give the knower the satisfaction of a panoramic view of reality.

The development of the sciences and of philosophy has led to great disappointments, however. In spite of our technical ability, and also to some extent as a result of it, we are overwhelmed by a sort of dizziness. The bewildering extent of our possibilities for altering or even annihilating nature has stricken us with anxiety: we no longer feel safe from the outbreak of a madness that sows death and destruction instead of progress.

Anxiety about our own abilities is neither the only nor the most prominent symptom of the crisis of our culture. The confusion of the framework in which the West has felt at home for centuries is revealed most clearly in art. Noises from an electronically invoked wilderness, formless forms and worn-out images, melodies, and ideas, but also tentative elements from which new formations may perhaps germinate, whirl around in a void that looks for direction. A hundred years ago, Nietzsche proclaimed that our culture was dying, along with the "values" sanctioned by its "God"; by now the awareness of this dying has trickled down into the sentiments and opinions of most intellectuals. A general anxiety with regard to meaning, superficial ways of talking about the slaying of human life, a sort of inability to engage in long-lasting alliances, and a widespread relativism are just as symptomatic of that dying as is the faded figure of a positive religion that for almost two millennia was the basis and binding force for our culture's sanctions. *Media vita in morte sumus.* Modern science has overcome the plague, but we ourselves have mass murdered millions. Yet, even nuclear war is not our greatest threat: worse than that is the danger that we are no longer capable of having ideals that make our lives meaningful enough to die for it. If Western culture is declining toward its end, the concern of philosophy and the sciences for their foundations and methodological conditions has perhaps to be viewed as a symptom of that agony. The ever-renewed and ever-failing attempt to establish a secure and indisputable point of origin for all knowledge begins to look like an entrenched ritual; while we abhor it, we cannot give it up, because the modern ideal does not allow for any trust without proof or control.

A further sign of the exhaustion of the modern project is the stagnant formalism of our anthropological, ethical, and metaphysical considerations, particularly in philosophy. We cannot return to premodern times, but would it not be beautiful if we could justifiably abandon ourselves to a postmodern, enlightened and responsible naïveté? As long as no such "enlightenment" is in sight, a sustained reflection on our being drawn into metatheoretical reflections—a sort of meta-metatheory—threatens to turn our thinking into lamentation. But there *must* be reasons for hope.

II.

If we try to reflect on the quality of human life without indulging in methodological considerations, we discover quickly that it is impossible to start from a zero-point without any assumptions. From the beginning, we are already seduced by modern and postmodern convictions that have infiltrated our culture. They constitute the "modern view" of quality and life, and no one today can elude them entirely, even if we no longer genuinely believe in them. Modernity is no longer a criterion of truth, even though we can overcome it only with the greatest effort. Being involved in a crisis, we are capable only of a distant and critical appropriation. Through reflecting on the modern assumptions that press themselves on us, we are driven toward a groping, poorly tested postmodernity.

What I boldly call "the modern view" here is of course a problematical concept. An attempt to sketch it is necessarily selective and contestable, but it is hardly possible to situate ourselves if we do not engage at all in such an attempt. Aware of these qualifications, I offer the following suggestions for a diagnosis of the modern perspective.

In order to determine "the quality of life," we must make distinctions between the categories of non-living, living, and human realities, and discover a criterion for determining the quality of human life in general and of concrete lives in particular. In order to determine such a criterion, many authors appeal to the idea that human beings have many wants whose satisfaction, if not strictly necessary, is greatly desired.

Hunger can function as a paradigm for human needs—although, for the most part, it is seldom analyzed as *human,* radically and totally different from animal hunger. It consists of a felt emptiness, a lack that urges us to fulfill it. The goal of this urge or drive is a feeling of gratification and enjoyment which makes the urge cease or diminish. After some time, however, we feel it again, once the emptiness has returned. The recurrence of the drive is just as essential as the persistence of the wants in which it is rooted. The temporality of needy beings is characterized by an alternation of various kinds of lack and fulfillment. Without such a time, a life of needs would not even be thinkable.

By extending the concept of need to all the other dimensions of human striving, we interpret the whole of human existence as an individual economy of competing drives. The art of life, according to such a perspective, consists in harmonizing our hygienic, social, aesthetic, sporting, scientific, religious, financial, and other needs so that their respective fulfillments bring about the greatest possible total satisfaction. The question of happiness is then reduced to an economic problem when we can conceive of all human endeavors as variations on one theme: "need seeks satisfaction." The success of an individual life is then measured by the degree of satisfaction it achieves. In this framework, the question of quality is solved by conceiving all the goals of human desire as subclasses of one purpose: fulfillment or satisfaction. If it is possible to quantify particular satisfactions according to their volume and intensity (as is presupposed in many inquiries and ethical theories), the question of how much a human life is worth seems to be answerable. The highest value is then found in the maximum satisfaction of a person's combined needs for health, love, and gastronomic, artistic, or other kinds of pleasure. It goes without saying that this happiness lasts only as long as a person does not die. But we want immortal happiness. Should we calculate our chance of an early or late death to include it as a factor in our economy of wants?

Certain moralists have supposed that we should be able to give a universally applicable description of such maximal well-being or "happiness." Many people see comfort, status, love, sex, sports, music, and television as indispensable elements of human happiness. Few intellectuals, however, will defend the thesis that all persons must conform to one model for the conduct of life. According to a modern axiom, all individuals have a right to decide for themselves what they consider to be most worthy of desire. This right is even taught as an obligation: every individual is responsible for the way he arranges his life and pursues its unfolding. However, choosing a pattern of values and conduct that is strictly one's own is not simple within a pluralistic culture like ours. Ever since the great voyages of discovery, the historical sciences, and cultural anthropology made us familiar with an immeasurable diversity of views about wants and happiness, we wander lost in an immense museum where everything can be experienced while nothing is forced on us.

If we are unmoored from all traditions, the task of choosing the best way of life from the available list of samples becomes difficult. Even then, we do not solve the question of a satisfying life through a completely independent choice made from a neutral point of view, but rather by seeking connection with one of the few models the recent past has made familiar to us through education. The idea of an autonomous choice out of the totality of all the possibilities of life is a modern fiction; although it has some philosophical significance, it is neither a description of the facts nor very helpful as a guiding principle for choosing one's own lifestyle.

Thirty years ago, those intellectuals who propagated a world revolution inspired by Marx rooted themselves in an old tradition, in which Jewish, Greek, Christian, Roman, Germanic, modern, and bourgeois elements were clearly perceptible. Today, as well, those who advocate a new form of inwardness would not be able to do so if they were not inspired by contact with former texts and ways of life. Our freedom is borne from streams of life that we have not invented; it would not even come into play (making choices available) if it were not receptive to suggestions through which the past still touches it. Taking initiative includes a fundamental capacity for acceptance. Without gratitude, there can be no hope.

Good taste is needed in order to recognize the worthwhile elements of prominent traditions, even if their worth, as nonsuperficial, is deeply hidden. A truly "autonomous" choice would in fact be based on an uncivilized nature of brute feelings; thus it would generate only barbarism.

A plea for the enduring worth of European, humanistic, and

Christian traditions must not degenerate into a colonialistic depreciation of other histories, especially since our knowledge of them is poor. Neither must our plea be misunderstood as advocating traditionalism and passivity. Receptivity to the hidden power of traditions is entirely different from passive surrender to the patterns of a past out of which we have now emerged. Authentically reexperiencing powerful elements of a history whose retrieval can revitalize our life requires openness. This, however, presupposes escaping from the narcissism of immediate wants that cling to the all-too-familiar. Between the fearful image of enslavement and the heroism of a stoic autarky, we seek a more modest form of freedom, one that combines love for the earth with an original transformation of proven possibilities for living.

III.

The interpretation of human striving for happiness as an economy of wants, arranged by autonomous individuals according to their own wishes, adheres to a model that plays an important role not only in social theories, but also in countless practices of modern society. In the absence of universally valid purposes such as might be discerned from a divine plan or from human nature, individual choices take the place of God's or Nature's or Humanity's will. Everyone's right to realize personal well-being according to one's own plan is limited only by the same right that belongs to everyone else. The autonomous life projects of all individuals must be harmonized if we want to prevent a total anarchy. Within the given framework, this can occur only if all individuals recognize each other's autonomy and the necessity of a mutual restriction of rights. This makes contract and convention the foundations of society. All social relations and the cohesion of the society as a whole are then founded in contractual relations, i.e., in the factual agreement of the choices of those concerned. With this, any nonchosen union disappears from the horizon, so that even loyalty and all forms of solidarity are interpreted and practiced as pure contracts.

The reduction of human sociality to an economy of needs makes contractual dealings possible because it sees all sorts of satisfaction as varieties of one homogeneous value. As "values," these varieties can be compared and exchanged. Money is the paradigmatic measure for the happiness of this kind of society. In a society that is governed by the triumvirate of *needs, autonomy,* and *contract,* everything is for sale, even love, science, and art—even religion, if it is consumed as a possibility for satisfaction.

In a situation of abundance, the mutual limitations of individual freedom and rights are not strongly felt. In the wealthy regions of the West, a standard pattern of individual well-being developed after 1945 and very quickly came to be thought of as a kind of birthright. A decent dwelling, a car, a refrigerator, a washing machine, a color television, etc., symbolize what is commonly accepted in our time as the concretization of a universal right to well-being. Thanks to the prevailing prosperity and the idea of a certain equality, the fundamental right that belongs to everyone's human existence has been interpreted as claim to a specific pattern of life. If the latter is seen as an absolute right, we experience every possible infringement on it as a flagrant injustice. We will then oppose anyone who would meddle with our status. Within the individualistic framework of an economy of needs, it does not matter who encroaches on my rights. Even unborn children are then easily seen as enemies and treated as such. Fortunately, the modern idea of freedom and right is, in general, still fundamental enough to protect the weak, the handicapped, and the elderly against the greed of those who seek the fulfillment of their own desires at any cost. Fortunately, we are generally decent enough to recognize that a society of sheer competition is evil. However, the tendency to identify the fulfillment of life with a comfortable prosperity does not necessarily make life more joyful. The absolutization of prosperity leads to bitterness when prosperity recedes and to disappointment even when affluence continues. Is there a way to relativize comfort and want, so that we can take them seriously without making them the highest standards of quality?

IV.

Needs cannot function as the criterion for judging the "quality" of lives and meanings admired by modern or premodern traditions. The internal conflicts of our own needs and the incompleteness that accompanies every possible satisfaction as a sort of melancholy aura stand in need of a more radical orientation which they cannot give on their own. If it is true that human beings exceed their dependence on needs, and that, in spite of all satisfactions, we keep searching for something else, "greater," "deeper," "more radical" than satisfaction, then the true quality of life must be sought in the direction of another meaning. That meaning is then more necessary or "needed" than the stilling of our needs. The desire for that meaning can be awakened through experiences of misery, but also through a basic disappointment that accompanies all comfort and success.

From Plato and Plotinus, via Gregory of Nyssa, Augustine, Bonaventure, Ruusbroec and Teresa to Nietzsche, Kafka and Becket, innumerable specialists in the experience of life have described human existence as an incessant search for a meaning that transcends satisfaction. Their experience is repeated even now in many forms—for example, in the despair of those who cannot bear the lack of an ultimate meaning, or in the diffuse uneasiness of the many who console themselves with all sorts of gratifications without finding peace, or in the passion of following mysterious tracks toward some dimension or goal that is unknown though powerfully present through attraction. Both the tormented and the serene forms of this experience point to something that cannot be understood in terms of economy, hedonism, or calculation.

How shall we name the impulse that does not coincide with any of our needs, since it reaches further and never comes to an end? "Desire" is a good candidate for indicating the profound dynamism that we cannot halt but necessarily practice, although narcissism knows countless tricks to bind us to less profound purposes.

Desire for Meaning is something other than the need for quality. The structure of the desire that we are is not that of an emptiness to be filled up nor of a hunger that can be satisfied. Desire does not terminate in a fulfillment or definite conclusion; rather it is an affection that deepens by getting closer to the Desired. The intensity of this sort of "hunger" grows in direct proportion to the "fulfillment" that it receives. To approach what this desire is about is simultaneously to discover that it necessarily remains far off and hidden. Here discovering and finding cannot be possession, but only an intensified experience of being fascinated by something that is at once offered and withdrawn. The affection that keeps a human life in motion makes it impossible to resist the tendency—beyond all needs and satisfactions—toward a meaning that opposes every form of ownership. The experience of a meaning that cannot be captured in any combination of satisfactions casts a new light on the needs that rule us. Desire breaks through all levels of human need and into all the articulations of its affectivity; it is probed and tested in ownership and enjoyment, work, love, and freedom, but none of these fully responds to it; it cannot adore any one of them. We cannot do without such concretizations, but neither can they bring us to a standstill.

If the desire for an ultimate meaning is the main theme of a human life, the schema of self-unfolding-through-fulfillment loses its compelling force. No one may minimize the hunger of the actually hungry or the poverty of the destitute. But there is no hope of a radically meaningful life for poor or rich if the level of needs remains the most radical for them. Death and suffering remind us of the relativity of satisfaction. The certainty of death cannot be an argument for hating life, however. But it can stir a reflection that transcends the dimension of satisfaction by retaining it while deepening it. Satisfaction does not coincide with Meaning, even though the two cannot be separated.

V.

All of this can easily provoke objections and irritation. Even if it is true that desire does not coincide with the totality of needs, is an argument that defends the primacy of desire not more at home within a discussion between religions or worldviews than in a philosophical or scientific forum? Does my discourse not advertise a dangerous mixture of literary genres that should remain separate? What does the practice of scholarship have to do with a description of experiences so intimate that respectable academics would rather keep them to themselves? Must we not defend ourselves against an invasion by religious points of view just as much as against a politicizing of the academy, which was so impetuously proclaimed some decades ago?

Such objections would go without saying if academic practice could, without losing its human character, be dissociated from the fundamental motives that govern our lives. The modern ideal of an encyclopedic knowledge that is both fundamental and comprehensive can be criticized in many ways, and the ideal of a complete harmony between theory, affectivity, and praxis may be too high for us, but one thing seems undeniable: scholarship that is important for the quality of human life cannot be allowed to separate itself completely from the lived experience of life itself. It cannot and should not entirely avoid the influence of an orientation and style of life from which its scholarly practice emerges. The axiom that science and philosophy should not be concerned with the deepest motives of the soul is a modern naïveté.

The emancipation of knowing and doing from their subjection to human and pseudo-divine authorities is an achievement for which the world may be grateful to the modern West. The price that we have paid for it is a temporary division between the secular sciences, politics, and arts on one side, and the bulwarks advanced by traditions of religion, theology, and metaphysics on the other side. These bulwarks have stayed outside the main play of modern culture for several centuries, so that their words and deeds began to sound "supernatural," reactionary, and bombastic. Their powerless moralism testifies to a chasm that made it even more difficult for modern culture to link its own significance with the question of ultimate meaning. A radical perspective on life was left to subjective and individual decisions, but these, in their turn, elicited reinforcements of authoritarian dogmatism on the other side. In the political and juridical sphere, we have seen from the regimes of Hitler, Stalin and Mao Tse-tung what a division between the state-sponsored university and humanism means. In the religious domain we observe a fierce conflict between the presumptuousness of spiritual dictators who try to regulate the life of their subordinates down to the most intimate details, and the individualistic appeal to private consciences that draw all their wisdom from their isolation. Modern morality has presented us with well-intended versions of collectivism, but these too have died of their own poverty concerning the question of meaning. As long as we chop human life into pieces by consigning science, religion, morality, art, and common sense to separate compartments, we should not count on a healing of our culture.

Whoever enjoys the earth as hidden presence of the ultimately desired, without however grasping or commanding it, bears witness to Meaning. Being moved in such a way points to something that is at once earthly yet indefinable, since it causes all human movement, but eludes every delimitation. Within the horizon that accompanies such a movement, our needs and satisfactions change, as do also the freedom and rights that we claim. Natural and bodily processes, labor and consumption, economy and justice, humanitarian plans and calculations, solitary and shared pains are then borne (and to a certain extent made bearable) by a fundamental disposition of receptivity. This changes our way of feeling and speaking, for example with regard to the burdens of work, the pains of suffering and dying, the welcoming of as-yet-unborn persons, and the threat of collective annihilation.

VI.

The character of science and philosophy also changes in the light
of Desire. The modern spirit makes place for another inspiration
that has more affinity with premodern moods and ways of seeing.

If we use the term "ethics" for the study of purposes and
norms whereby human behavior should properly be led, and the
term "metaphysics" for a fundamental reflection on the nature
and the grounds of reality, then every science that reflects on its
place within the human universe certainly has an ethical and a
metaphysical aspect. Even though we can hardly avoid specialization and concentration on isolated, fragmentary projects, the
unity of the sciences with each other and with the life-experi-
ment of which they are moments lies as an inevitable ideal within
the unity of human life, and the pursuit of this ideal cannot avoid
the normative aspects that are inseparable from that unity. The
search for a new coherence of the sciences in the perspective of a
radical meaning might be stimulated by the following remarks.

The manner in which modern humanity has tried to arrange a
meaningful world can be characterized as a technical-theoretical
project that has determined nature and society by observation,
experimental manipulation, calculation, and planning on the
basis of human needs. Need has become *the* yardstick for the values that should be attributed to the various phenomena of
nature and culture. The noblesse of the modern culture lies in its
ideal of universal justice, but for the content of justice it appeals
to needs and satisfaction, rarely to other kinds of meaning. Insofar as personal behavior and group relations are calculable and
plannable, the social sciences have rightly taken their example
from the model of the natural sciences, but again: where do we
find human goals that make our lives better than comfortable?
The modern project runs up against its limits as soon as it
attempts to subordinate individuals and masses to political or
economic, profane or religious autocracies. What humans *qua*

humans are and desire cannot be explicated or even observed by natural sciences; it is concealed from the scientific manner of looking and understanding. (Obviously I am not giving a psychological description here of the motives that run through the head of this or that sociologist or psychologist. Every attempt to typify a culture or one of its parts makes general pronouncements about the anonymous orientations to which individuals can be subject even *without* being conscious of them.)

The consolation of art and literature, with which the "soft" sciences occupy themselves, expresses another relation of the person to existence than that of mastery and exploitation. Mathematicians and physicists, too, can look at reality in an aesthetic way, but insofar as they do this, are they not much more heirs of Plato and the pre-Socratics than of modernity? Lingering with the aesthetic, verbal and musical aspects of reality can awaken both delight and horror. Many shocking artworks symbolize the difficult situation in which humans and history find themselves. Inhospitable voids and forced ugliness intensify our awareness of who and what and how we are and are not here and now; they reveal a "disharmony of spheres" over which we have no power.

Aesthetic products can be consumed as if they existed merely for someone's self-satisfaction. The meaning of art, however, lies in the observable or resonating communication of experiences in which a recipient (who is not a consumer) recognizes what the author (who is not a "maker," since that author is just as much a recipient) suggests to him.

Though modern science has separated itself from religious allegiances, its project is still animated by a moral intention: concerned with Humanity, many scientists focus on the life quality of individuals and societies. The worth of human beings cannot be produced or calculated, but some idea of it orients all activities, including those of the scientists. The fact that other persons exist resists any project that would reduce persons to links within a manipulable system. The "worth" of the other is entirely invisible to the observation of calculating eyes.

When I encounter someone, I can capture this person in the network of my needs. I then see him as a supplement that I can use or enjoy for myself. Yet, insofar as he is another, he eludes me: I ignore his self, because he dissolves in the elements that I appropriate to myself during the conversation.

The beginning of a moral relation lies in the discovery that a human being is not material for anyone's self-satisfaction, but something wholly different: an irreducible response to my desire for an irresistible core of meaning. Every encounter is an infringement on my spontaneous inclination to make it "mine." Thus every successful encounter is an awakening, because the discovery of another's dignity changes the face of the world. All phenomena and activities, scientific ones included, receive an irreducible orientation through the existence of others whose compelling appearance cannot be reduced to "values," but can only be respected or loved.

The moral shock presented by the existence of other humans cannot be the last answer in our search for meaning. Even though we realize that one cannot be good without dedication to others, and although we are prepared to practice such a dedication, a decisive question remains: what do I have to offer to another? In what does consist the meaning that makes the other's life, or mine, successful? Even mutual servitude of everyone to everyone is not a conclusive answer, since it does not yet tell us what is ultimately good for those we want to serve.

Working for a just and less miserable world, social criticism and idealism, helping the poor, and other sorts of care for persons bear witness to a moral devotion that can motivate even the practice of science. Basic needs for food, clothing, and shelter appeal to us; justice is one of the few virtues that even modern persons deem self-evident. But if a person cannot live by food, clothing, shelter, comfort, work, science, art, and love *alone*, then the question continues to obsess us: wherein does true success or failure lie? What is the decisive quality beyond all qualities?

With these questions, we come directly into the religious dimension, a dimension that cannot be superseded, certainly not by science. The meaning on which the success or failure of human existence depends can no more be captured by a definition than it can be commanded by prescriptions or dogmas. To know this Meaning is to seek it as a "sought" that never stops being sought. It seems to withdraw continually as we approach it, but in doing so it fascinates ever more intensely. The most radical receptivity is appropriate with regard to this Meaning: it waits and welcomes while engaging in earthly ways of communication, science, politics, art, and positive religion. The search for the Sought is achieved in many ways: not only in religious confessions and practices, but also in searching forms of *skepsis* and atheism.

If human needs and desires cannot be separated from a fundamental orientation toward ultimate meaning, and if the practice of science reconnects the experiment that we necessarily undertake with our own lives, then the sciences need a religious sensibility to get in touch with life as it is lived. There is a widespread fear that an alliance of science with religion or theology would contaminate the objectivity of autonomous investigations by smuggling in the unscientific influence of ecclesiastical, biblical, or historical authorities. Quite a lot could be said about the alleged absence of arguments from authority in modern philosophy and science, but let us concentrate on the main argument that is brought up against the feared mixing.

Positive sciences undeniably have a less direct connection with the dimension of metaphysical and religious radicality than does philosophy. Since its task is to ask radically about the why and the how of reality as it presents itself, philosophical thinking is necessarily concerned with the fundamental dimensions of existence. However, positive sciences also contain whole pieces of philosophy (if only the implicit assumptions of their methods) so that every scientific theory borders on philosophical questions that are the explicit concerns of such disciplines as anthropology, ethics, social philosophy, epistemology, and metaphysics. As the intermediary practice of thinking on the basis of precisely described experiences, philosophy can mediate between the sciences and theology, on the condition that the latter does not confine itself to a philological, historical, and pastoral-scientific explication of positive religions but also interprets and evaluates these in their relations to the deepest mystery that attunes humans and reality to one another.

Although a thousand misunderstandings lie in wait here, I gladly defend the thesis that the most radical form of science and philosophy tangentially coincide with the most radical form of theology. The thesis sounds scandalous and needlessly sensational. However, it need not be so. Augustine and Aquinas, for example, found this view completely normal and necessary. However much modern philosophers prided themselves on the autonomy of their method, they, too, confirmed this thesis by their practice. Not a single modern thinker known to me has demonstrated the ideal of a completely autonomous system of truth, and nearly all the classics, including those of modern times from Descartes to Hegel, propose some theory of the absolute and ultimate. No thinking can deny that it is and remains rooted in prephilosophical experiences of a specific affective, imaginative, linguistic, moral, and religious character, which no allegedly autonomous reflection can completely recoup. If we understand theology as a rigorous reflection that brings to the fore and interprets what is essential to human reality on the basis of expressions and traditions in which Jews, Christians, Muslims, Hindus, Buddhists, atheists, and humanists pass on their deepest experiences with human existence and history, then it appears impossible to construe a chasm between a profound theology and a profound philosophy. Such a chasm is certainly impossible for those who are conscious of the unavoidable receptivity that links all thought to particular patterns, terminologies, habits, and histories. By denying the influence of traditions and prejudices, thinking does not make itself autonomous; on the contrary, it falls into a naïve obedience to the orientations and ideologies that have determined the prevailing climate of "this time." All philosophies bear witness to some unreflected belief by which their authors let themselves be carried. The structure of an "unbelieving" thinking does not differ essentially from the structure of a self-critical theology that attempts as much as possible to change its traditional and authoritarian beginning-point into a justified self-concept.

For those who treat the complete autonomy of the sciences as an absolute criterion, the "ideological" character of philosophy can be a reason to banish it, along with theology, from the university. Others, who have followed no less persistently and more thoroughly the modern motto of radical self-justification, will, on the other hand, plead for the preservation of philosophy and theology in the heart of the university. The condition they pose for this preservation is that these disciplines not be led by political or diplomatic maneuvers, but give evidence of a genuine ethos of scholarship by presenting thorough and, if needed, merciless arguments for their validity. A discipline that does not concern itself with the justification of its theoretical, affective, and practical presuppositions is too naïve to be taken seriously by an academic forum. This remark applies just as much to scientists who imagine themselves safe because they think their foundations are beyond scrutiny. *A fortiori*, we close our ears to political, journalistic, or religious voices that impose specific edicts on us without being prepared for a discussion about the rational quality of their assertions and authority.

IV. Meaning and Transcendence

T o be open for meaning is to be sensitive to a radical mystery that lies at the heart of everything. Human existence is a desiring and a striving—but for what? This question and the attempt to answer it remain with us our whole lives. We do not find a conclusive answer, not because there is no answer or because the question and the striving are meaningless, but because every discovery reaches beyond what has been discovered, inviting us to seek further and discover more fully. The meaning of a life is never completely known, and much of its why remains hidden; no word of wisdom is definitive, as long as death (and with it the death of our knowledge and understanding) has not come to pass.

Does desire drive us toward a goal, as if life were merely a preparation for "the real thing" that can only come after life, in the "end time" or "eternity"? All conceptions that see human life as a preparation (for example, as a work to be honored after its completion) operate within a teleological schema that subordinates the meaning of birth, growing up, learning to be human, and death to a final meaning that would lie in another, higher or more complete reality in the future. The world of our experience would point toward another world that awaits us if we conduct ourselves rightly in this lower and ephemeral world. As long as we have not yet died, we would have to be content with a world that is only a glimmer of what is yet to come. Whether someday we are to be lifted above this world (by our own efforts or otherwise) would depend on the way we are now living our lives.

This division into two worlds, an historical present and a transhistorical future or ideal "hereafter," structures many myths. Mythical time can even be characterized by it. One could interpret this structure as a metaphor for the simultaneity of two orientations: the historical present and the imagined future beyond death together constitute, then, one indivisible human history. We live at once "here below" and "there above." The deepest desire orients us to the pure and immortal core of reality that invites us to cleanse and sublimate finite existence.

If human beings live in two worlds, they are divided. Their chief task, then, consists in developing ways of life that subordinate their "lower" cravings to a higher calling. Radical desire makes human beings into seekers of the true good that attracts them from behind and above the fulfillments of their needs and cravings.

Is our desire for meaning a striving for a goal above and beyond the aims of our cravings? The answer depends on what we understand by "goal," "desiring," "needs," and "craving."

The desire that permeates a human life is *not* a need. As we have seen, this is evident from the fact that it cannot be appeased, but grows and becomes more desirous the more it comes closer to the desired. What is desired does not fill or satisfy in the way food can satisfy. Desire is not a hunger, but a longing for *Meaning* that cannot be stilled. Meaning does not bring our desire to rest, and desire is structured differently from a void that tries to annul itself. When the desired and our desire draw nearer to one another, this proximity deepens and aggravates the suffered emptiness. Progress in the search of Meaning strengthens the heart and makes it grow in trust, but it also extends its desolation and deepens the night that surrounds the mystery. In the desert, the air is pure and the clouds are full of fire. Light and darkness, desert and paradise, anticipation and achievement, desiring and embracing go together and do not abolish one other.

Desire determines our mood even before we can think or choose. It brings us into an affective disposition that colors the corporeal processes and the encounters we undergo. We allow the phenomena and events to affect us in various ways for which we have become open, but we also play an active role in the interplay. Our experiences are responses to occurrences that let us get "in the mood." Learning how to desire is the task. A human being is an entity that hopes for a good mood. "Transcendence" is another name, be it a cooler one, for the most profound affectivity.

What does a good mood have to do with the ultimate meaning? What is the meaning of the mood we experience? Who or what is the desired? Does it (or he or she) have any other name than "the Desired" or "the Sought"? Some philosophers have contended that we do not know what or who God is, but can and must affirm that he is. But how can anyone contend that "He (or She or It) *is*" without thinking anything specific by pronouncing the word "He" (or "She" or "It")? The intention of that surprising assertion was apparently to distinguish between two different sorts of "knowledge." Knowing what is ultimately desired is not to know a thing or a being, not even to know a highest Something or supreme Being. Surely, if there is a highest Reality, it does stand above all other realities, but such a summit is "too small" to be the answer to the question of what we are striving for. To whom or what is our "heart" directed? A highest Being still looks far too much like other beings. Even if it is the ground, the wellspring, the foundation, and the crown of them all, such a being is somehow homogeneous with other realities that we can apprehend through representations or concepts and contain as entities or principles in our consciousness. The desired is not less than a supreme being or the allness of being, but at the same time it is "nothing of all that." It is radically otherwise than everything we can make familiar by giving it a place and a function in our world or mind; it necessarily is and remains "strange" and "unknown." And yet "It" is what is most familiar to our desire and, as the secret that elicits our search, a blinding light (and thus the deepest darkness) that has lodged itself in our most originary awareness.

Acquaintance with the Unknown, which or who eludes representation and conceptualization, is the most basic and certain of all affirmations. It precedes all feeling, imagining, thinking, and striving. At the same time, it causes uncertainty, since it eliminates and denies all attempts to grab hold of it through images, concepts, theses, works, and symbols. As the negation of "all that"—and thus some kind of not-a-thing or No-thing—the Sought overwhelms anyone who, out of anxiety, seeks salvation in Something (a grand Architect, an almighty Father, a moving Cause or Unmoved Mover, etc.) that we could capture in a thought or image. The anxiety that is the reverse of our desire is unbearable unless that "Nothing" makes itself felt as a Meaning that, neither something nor nothing, is otherwise and "more" than everything whose presence we can define or contain.

If "the highest" were a being, a collection of beings, or the universe itself, we would desire a synthesis of the higher *and* the lower, in which case the desire for God would be merely a *part* of what we desire, *or* we would have to choose between the higher and the lower, in which case God and "the lower" would be enemies, as many atheists suppose. However, since God is "Nothing," a dualism that plays God against the universe is impossible. Thus Desire eludes the division between a religious world above (or "heaven") and an historical world below that should be subordinated to it. Differences of level between higher and lower (in quality, style, beauty, power, spirit, etc.), as well as the problem of harmonizing them, retain their force, but The Desire is not one of the many desires, tendencies, or cravings. The Meaning to which it is directed does not exclude any single meaning because it is something *other* than the synthesis of all meanings. Thanks to it, anxiety (which must be experienced in order to avoid definitively settling into the world of higher and lower) can change into hope. Gratitude "knows" that "my All," just like Nothing, is only a provisional name for the Sought.

A perspective that seeks salvation in a higher world (for example, in a supreme Being "above" the finite) is idolatrous, since it identifies the sought with a *part* of the universe. A perspective that identifies the Absolute with the synthesis of all the finite is just as idolatrous, even though its god is greater, since it is "more comprehensive" than that of the first perspective. Whoever cannot get beyond the highest being or a universe that includes all beings does not achieve transcendence. The transcendence of Desire directs us from the outset toward a Meaning that, neither high nor low, is the mystery concealed in all the highs and lows that we experience. The Sought gives itself to be "known" because it wants to be "in" and "with" and "as" everything given, without giving up the gratuitous freedom of its giving. To enjoy without greedily annihilating the givenness of the given is to be thankful. The "Nothing" that jars us from all our apparent security and the "All" that fulfills us are provisional names for the Inexpressible that escapes all names, without however dissolving into anonymity. We recover from an all-too-known (commercial, judicial, fatherly, motherly) God through strong doses of atheism, but secularization is not more than a halfway measure, only an introduction to the search.

V. The Relevance of
Natural Theology

The term "natural theology" evokes a whole constellation of ideas. Anyone who takes up this expression without a critical distance, directly defending or opposing a *theologia naturalis,* is already caught in a specific program.

Ever since the 18th century, "nature," to which natural theology appeals, has been contrasted with the positivity of historical religions, especially the Christian religion. The discovery of a "natural religion" (parallel to that of a natural morality, a natural law, and a natural society) was a theoretical move with many theoretical, practical and affective benefits.

The diversity of cultures, which had become known through the reconnaissance of the globe and the study of history, could be surveyed and explained via the concept of "nature." The different religions, moralities, and systems of law were understood as variations on one constant theme that underlay its historical performances. Human "nature" as an inherent pre- or ahistorical reality could be characterized by its pre- and ahistorical morality, religion, and metaphysics; the variants represented by the different cultures were accidental. It was even possible to reject every religion, and particularly the Christian one, as a deformation of the single, unadulterated, essential, self-evident, and pure religion on which everyone should agree. In the strategy of anti-Christian critics, "nature" became a polemical concept and "back to nature" a call to purification from historical distortions. Others, who believed in "Progress," conceived of human nature with its religion and morality as a seed that had to develop itself, via a variety of peoples and times, into the present-day richness and a future completion. For them too, natural religion was the heart of the matter since they saw history as the self-unfolding of a "primitive" nature that remained fundamentally the same through all its changes.

Theologians and apologists used the contrast between "natural" and "positive" to demonstrate that revelation has not descended all at once from heaven, but is linked to a knowledge that human beings (even in primitive conditions) naturally possess. They presented the Christian religion as a rationally believable, even plausible, though God-given elaboration of that natural knowledge.

Anyone who uses the concept of "natural religion" in the given sense relies on a specific understanding of history and its significance for life and society. A critique of the theories for which the concept of "natural religion" is basic will have to include a critique of their concept of history.

The motivation for the idea of a natural religion was not sheerly theoretical. It emerged in a situation where many enemies of the Christian churches championed a new consciousness of freedom. Human autonomy, interpreted in a specifically modern way, implies that every individual must, in principle, be able to rationally justify his or her basic decisions and convictions. As soon as I consider it unworthy of an adult to submit to the authority of a tradition, I owe myself a complete justification, and I have an inalienable right to it. Such a self-justification consists in a logically conclusive explanation of valid experiences. *If* religion is to be legitimated in this way, all normal individuals must be able to justify for themselves their inmost convictions in relation to God. Such a legitimation cannot rely on what others say; thus it can rely neither on the authority of priests or prophets, nor on the authority of visionaries, apostles, or eyewitnesses who claim to know what we do not know through experiences or arguments of our own. Current experience and thought must suffice to establish the essential truths that give the ultimate orientation to each individual life. "Tradition" or "privileged authority" are no acceptable foundation, because they compromise our personal autonomy where it matters most.

The legitimacy of a religion is guaranteed if every human being has the opportunity to discover independently the core of the truth to which this religion adheres. We must be able to do this solely on the basis of our own capabilities, not through the pronouncements of other persons or traditions. The concept of "nature" thus safeguards the sovereignty of personal freedom. According to this interpretation, "natural religion" does not primarily mean a religion that belongs to human nature, but rather a religion that can be discovered by any person independently of traditions and history.

The modern fight for emancipation was not only a rejection of authority, but also, from the very beginning, an indictment against falsification. At first, this fight was conducted in a relatively harmless manner: many intellectuals fulminated against priestly deceitfulness, and particularly against the Jesuits, since they represented the greatest cultural power among priests. Later, the alleged untruthfulness of the existing religion was attacked by more radical means; religiosity was then interpreted as a symptom of unconscious forms of alienation.

"Nature" was advanced by Rousseau and others as an instrument to criticize and purify the decayed culture, including its religion. Gradually, however, "nature" itself crumbled and lost its religious, metaphysical, and moral connotations. The normative significance of nature as a criterion of purity was despiritualized. "Nature" became synonymous with organic life, unconscious

affective drives, vital energy, matter, or other physically determined substance. Naturally, with this reduction one of the traditional meanings of "God" was lost.

The concept of "nature" received the death-blow when it
became dominated by a total historicization. At first (with Hegel,
for example), history was still conceived as the development of a
transhistorical process, but this conception died when every thesis, every theme, and every constant came to be seen as an expo-
nent of a specific historical formation, which (like all other
historical formations) was understood as essentially contingent.

With the abolishment of a transhistorical, "natural" standard, it
was believed that the possibility of falsification also disappeared.
Radical nihilism makes any evaluation impossible. The only
remaining critique is an investigation of the inner coherence or
incoherence of contingent structures. And even this critique is
perhaps no longer possible. For on what grounds can one demand
coherence? Is not this requirement also a contingency, something
that depends on the biases and views of whoever interprets?

"Nature," as the universal and neutral basis of religion, morality, justice, and philosophy, was invented to save the core of Western European culture through critique and reorientation.
However, it did not prove solid enough to withstand the under-
mining effects of an extended critique that increasingly robbed
nature of its purpose and necessity. The crumbling of Western
humanism began by rejecting history and ended with the explo-
sion of what was, at first, conceived as its core. History tri-
umphed, but at the cost of its own meaning.

The God of natural religion is the God of natural theology; it is
the God of those who want to decide, on their own reckoning,
what they must think and do about the most fundamental concerns of human life. In addition to his ahistorical character, this
God is defined by two other characteristics.

First, he is the Ground of all actuality and possibility, a
ground that must necessarily be thought if the principle of

ground possesses a universal validity and if reality is to be comprehended as the universe of all that is actual and possible. Some intellectuals polemicize in the name of this God against the Gods of the positive religions, while others claim to find here support for affirming the God of their belief; both tendencies, however, are subject to the same schema of thinking, in which a more radical and more genuine God cannot appear. Under the pressure of this schema, even the onto-theo-logical theologian cannot thematize the God of Abraham, Moses, and Jesus otherwise than as an illustration of the Ground that grounds everything.

The second characteristic of the God of 18th-century natural theology is his moralizing character. God is thought of as an extension of morality, as rewarder of good and punisher of evil, and thus as a judge who in judging confirms our "natural" judgment about good and evil by punishing and rewarding what through human knowledge or power occurs. The morality on which this doctrine of God is based is a special one: it cannot think of good and evil outside of their connection with happiness and unhappiness. Whoever is good *must* be happy. It is necessary, a question of justice, that those who act badly should become unhappy. God is needed in order to firmly establish this connection. Hence immortality is also an essential component of natural religion and its theology.

Thus the universe is understood in the light of a moral purpose: Justice—as a summary of just verdicts—is the word that stands above the temple of Reason. "Critique" has become the key word; the norm is *our* ("natural") concept of *merit*, God is the guarantor of the unbreakable relationship between moral goodness and happiness, evil and sorrow.[1]

Here several questions arise: is there an inner coherence between the two characteristics named here? Is an onto-theo-logy possible without the primacy of a specific morality and vice versa? Is a critique of onto-theo-logy *ipso facto* a critique of the moralism sketched above? If the first characteristic does not imply the second, we could identify the concept of "natural theology" with that of an ahistorical onto-theo-logy and leave out a critique of Western moralism. In that case it would be more or less accidental that the 18th-century form of natural theology is so moralistic, and we would be able to search for other, nonmoralizing forms of onto-theo-logy.

If both characteristics imply one another, we must search for what binds them together. Perhaps we must follow Nietzsche insofar as his criticism of religion was inseparable from his criticism of morality. Does the bridge between morality and religion lie in the notion of a *Hinterwelt,* a necessary presupposition for both the natural theology and the natural morality of the 18th century? Since the predominant moral demand of that epoch, the *right* to happiness as directly linked to a virtuous life, is not fulfilled in "this" world (which is held to be established fact, against the Stoics and Spinoza, who saw virtue as its own reward), the fulfillment must be given in another world. The Beyond is conceived as a world in which everything happens as we think it actually *should* occur in this world. The ruler who sits behind the whole procession of affairs is a superhuman judge. He is not only perfectly just, but he also can realize everything he wants. Since he, in the end, fulfills the demands of our moral system, in which the good is identical with just retribution, we can count on the vindication of all actions through pleasures and rewards and pains. The highest being, in which all of reality is grounded, is the result of a legitimating thinking. The self-vindication of the subject of natural theology is at the same time a vindication of God: a *theo-dicy.*

Is the theoretical justification of natural theology as such related to or even identical with the vindication of the moral view of the world? Perhaps the inclination toward right and vindication (the fundamental conviction that everyone may rightfully *demand* freedom and happiness) is the real motive of onto-theo-logy in its modern form. Perhaps the moralistic attitude that arises from this demand is a much deeper root of the current atheism than is the will to dominate the world through technical power. Whatever the case, in what follows I will chiefly direct my attention to the onto-theo-logical structure of natural theology.

Every critique of natural theology must begin by recognizing its positive contributions. All serious attempts to show philosophically the religious component latent in the human essence deserve sympathy and consideration. However much the various forms of onto-theo-logy may deserve doubts and criticism, we cannot rise above it through ignorance or superficiality. More profound thinking might be required, as is normal for the most radical of all intellectual enterprises, but avoidance is all too cheap. Even if thorough investigations fail to disclose the foundations they seek, their orientation suggests a more radical thinking to overcome their failures.

Hence to prescind, in a fideistic way, from all philosophizing about God is a misdirected approach. Some of those who take this approach see themselves as agreeing in philosophy with atheists or agnostics. If they are right, God and religion are not at home in philosophy, but belong to another domain: that of belief or theology. Yet, as far as theology is concerned, how can it unfold without encountering the thought of those philosophers who have pondered the relation of human beings to God? Would fideism still allow philosophy to reflect on the most relevant questions or would it see such as arrogance or even idolatry? As if theology itself were safe from such vices! *If* radical thinking is possible, it reaches out toward God. If not, believing and thinking lack a common horizon. But what kind of dualism do we then uphold? This certainly makes it easier to understand why our culture no longer knows any great thinkers about God and religion: the fideistic division between religion and philosophy makes both philosophy of *religion* and theological *thinking* impossible.

This apology for thinking about religion does not imply that God could be an "object" or even a "concept." The flight into fideism can be understood as an aversion to every philosophy that tries to comprehend the God of faith. But such philosophies are already condemned by their own *philosophical* "concept" of God. They do not know what they want to think.

Over against fideism, the rationalistic conception of philosophy, theology and faith identifies thinking with conceptual comprehension or domination. However, not only Kant, but also Plato, Plotinus, Augustine, Thomas, Descartes, Nietzsche and Heidegger have made it clear that thinking is not the same as grasping; it is a kind of reaching out, through exploring and surmising, toward that which remains impenetrable, although all light and enlightenment ultimately depend upon it. Beyond being, beyond the ideas, is that which is in itself the most clear, while for us it is the darkest: the One to which all beings owe their truth and their being; an "Idea" that cannot be grasped, since it radiates more light than all the "objects" and ideas of the universe can capture.

It is not true that Western onto-theo-logy can be dismissed by a critique of its conceptuality. In its summits, its reaching for grounds (its "archeology") does not culminate in attempts to master the universe through the concept of a cause or final ground, but rather in the admiration of a unique referent that cannot be grasped.[2] Comprehension of beings is possible thanks to an obscure awareness of something different from their being, and the ultimate horizon of this awareness cannot be made into the penultimate; it is the One that is the genuine beginning. We cannot comprehend a genuine beginning, because that would assume something prior, at least a horizon within which it can appear. We can think the ultimate or first, but we cannot grasp it. Not only is it too great for any concept or representation;[3] more fundamentally, we cannot reach behind the radical Beginning of everything. God is not a highest being within a horizon. If he were, he would not be God, but a being. He is the "horizon" itself.

The direction in which to seek God is beyond the limits of onto-theo-logy; he cannot be found "within the limits of mere reason," but only through a search that reaches out beyond any fence. For this search, it does not suffice to ameliorate the coherence of Western onto-theo-logy or to transcend it in a thought of

Being itself. The being of all beings (which, as being*s*, are finite) cannot be the ultimate, if it is true that prayer and religion are "natural" for human existence.

Critique of onto-theo-logical thinking needs a prephilosophical basis: a certain "knowledge" or "experience" through which God is already present, even though this "knowledge" cannot (yet) defend itself in a philosophical way. Without some form of religious experience or another, the question of God cannot come up, even in philosophy. Every critique of theology relies on a preceding awareness that is certain enough of itself to transcend the movement of thinking it criticizes. To transcend is to rise above, even though it is not yet clear what awaits us. But something of a direction and some appearance of new possibilities on the horizon are necessary if transcendence is to be something other than wistful self-delusion.

If we try to realize concretely what the "proofs for the existence of God" achieve, religious experience can reveal itself in the disappointment or boredom that those proofs bring about. In order to be fruitful for philosophy, religious experience must present itself in a serious engagement with philosophical theology, i.e., in a thinking that accepts the dangers of genuine seeking.[4]

For example, the ultimate disappointment that results from genuinely following the "cosmological" way toward the first and last Ground signifies that this way falls "too short": what is reached does not correspond to the God whom I "knew" in the mode of seeking. Even if someone asserts that "this is what everyone calls 'God,' "[5] this Ground is not equivalent to the living God who is present in our search by eliciting it.

Such a short-circuit is no reason to pose a contradiction between the God of Abraham and the God of philosophy. If the living God were to veil himself from every form of philosophy (and not only from the intractable *sophia* and *philosophia* with which Paul had such unhappy experiences), this would mean that philosophical reason would be essentially and necessarily godless.

Onto-theo-logy would then be an empty academic exercise and we would do better to choose between an atheistic philosophy or a nonphilosophical theology.

However, the contrast between the disappointing God of the "proofs" and a more true, actually sought God belongs *within* philosophy and is best considered there, where radicality of thinking is at home.

The living God attracts me through my desire. But if this is what I really and radically desire, it will not leave my reason cold. Reason and thinking are led on by a passion toward something that exceeds all proofs as much as desire surpasses all argumentation. Not only Plato's dialectic, but every form of onto-theology and all thinking about the being of beings points toward a "horizon" that, without being an "object," enables us to think and to be grateful for it.

In order to judge the moralizing character of natural theology, we can begin with a critique of morality. By unmasking the resentment of Western and "Christian" moralities, we can purify the perspective from which God should be approached. A more radical critique, however, is required to conquer the attempts to make moral paradigms into the ultimate itself. Such a critique flows out of a religious experience that cannot see God as a mere judge or justice as the ultimate good. "Gratuitous love," "grace," "giving," and "goodness" are more appropriate to name God. Desire transcends morality and right. With due respect and love for right and charity, desire hints in the direction of a giving that precedes demands.

Much is to be said and still more to be investigated about the significance of history for a philosophical search for God. How does "religious experience" relate to the history of the Jewish, Christian, and other religions that have given shape to our feeling, thinking, and striving? What is the significance of traditions, texts, and shared stories for thinking and rethinking about God?

I close with one more remark, which, though not yet reaching the heart of the matter, might indicate a direction. If we suppose that our situation is one of watching and waiting in a void that prevents us from mentioning God's name with sincerity, the interpretation of our experience somehow parallels the self-interpretation that many mystics have given of their spiritual aridity and nights.

The description of our situation as full of grief for the absence of Meaning indicates a future for Desire. Tentatively giving names to the Desirable, we risk to fall back on very familiar or senseless words, but some of these might function as harbingers of a new day. After the dawn, new experiences and words will be tested again and again. Is our readiness to re-examine what we will have found a sign of our advancement in the direction of the One whose presence is experienced in being (the) Sought?[6]

VI. RELIGION AND EXPERIENCE

The intention of this chapter is modest: it seeks to emphasize the importance of one formal element only, that of religious experience. This choice is not arbitrary, since experience is fundamental both for the life of religion and for a philosophical assessment of it. How experience relates to other elements of a religious life can be shown only in a well-developed theology or metatheology. The following, therefore, is not much more than a series of suggestions for such a theology.

Although the Christian religion exists as a social and historical fact, this does not mean that its only or primary concern is with a collective fate; rather, it is about the ultimate meaning of each one's individual life, although this individuality should not be isolated from the community. If "the church," "the people," and "history" are opposed to human individuality, we are forced to choose between the two as the highest reality. But either choice would result in an aporia: either we would neglect the essential sociality of human persons, or we would suppress their individual freedom through a collectivist conception that defines them in terms of their belonging together in one community.

While the gospel speaks to a "little flock" of individuals about their salvation, it also contains numerous expressions of the new Israel's unity. Augustine and many other authors concerned with religious life have stressed the relationship between God and "the (individual) soul,"[1] without intending thereby to exclude the soul's belonging to the communion of saints, but Western theology has often been plagued by individualistic tendencies, especially in the last centuries. We have begun to rediscover the social aspects of the Christian faith,[2] but this should not weaken our sensibility for the depth of personal experiences of intimacy with God, as expressed in the classics of our spiritual tradition.

An immanent interpretation of Christian doctrine can show how this doctrine is the conceptual elaboration of a Presence that is primarily experienced in a preconceptual intimacy. "All theory [without love] is gray," as Goethe's Mephistopheles said.[3] To pray the Magnificat is to believe the truth of creation and grace more profoundly than is possible for even the best dogmatics. Who would not agree that the mystical prose and poetry of Juan de la Cruz give a more convincing testimony to God's trinity than theological treatises that do not emerge from experience? Something similar is true of Christian practice. Primarily, it is neither about following laws and prescriptions nor about a tradition of morals and customs; it is first of all a prereflective and preprescriptive form of life, carried out in a specific way of relating to God, yourself, others, and the entire universe.

A philosophy of religion centered on experience meets with great difficulties, however: is not experience too subjective a basis? How are we to distinguish genuine from inauthentic experiences? Shouldn't we instead focus on behavior, rather than on feelings, moods, and intentions?

The rejection of all introspection by psychologists, the (quasi-) philosophical problems of our (well-ascertained) knowledge of "other minds," concerns about the impossibility of a "private language," and the psychoanalytical dismantling of all self-certainty betray a widespread anxiety. Aversion to inwardness poses serious epistemological problems; at best it continues, in its own way, the old moral and religious suspicions about imitation, illusion, inauthenticity and impurity that have accompanied the great literature of spiritual life. These suspicions deserve serious consideration, though not necessarily at the *beginning* of a philosophy of religion. Any consideration of the epistemological difficulties that accompany religious experience must presuppose the inner life we want to investigate. Such considerations should rely on accurate descriptions of the most authentic experiences. If these cannot be guaranteed, we must at least have some guidance at progressively replacing less authentic by more authentic ones. Just as the world is not a chimera simply because the wonder of its existence continues to surprise epistemologists, neither is it necessary (or perhaps even possible) to solve the epistemological problems that are raised by religion *before* we naively accept the indisputable fact that we understand each other when we speak about "inner" adventures and intimate experiences. This fact does not destroy, but includes our individual differences in understanding that make our communication so interesting.

A philosophy of (religious) experience must search for some criteria to distinguish the genuine from the fake, and the pure from the murky. A mere description of the factual experiences that "believers" (as well as others) have is not the kind of answer we are looking for. The results of psychological or sociological inquiries that only survey convictions or experiences of self-professed believers would not give us an insight into the basic experience(s) of authentic religion. Such studies present an overview of average factualities. However, religious experience is not simply a generalization of all phenomena that are called "religious." Induction and generalization cannot distinguish between genuine and fake instances of love, virtue, belief, behavior, and so on, if it is not guided by some standard by which to judge. Authentic or "true" religion is an "idea," that is, a reality that appears nowhere else than in empirical reality, while at the same time containing a criterion for evaluation of the empirical data.[4] It is a unity of existence and value, of *Sein* and *Sollen,* an ideal that does not float above reality and is not threatened by its empirical realization, because it constitutes the core of a life that experiences *itself* as striving for a more appropriate realization of its deepest meaning.

All experiences, but especially the experiences that occur on the level of a radical search for meaning, have the character of a self-examination and critical self-evaluation. Experience is not a state of mind, but an experiment. It is part of an overall movement through which I discover, unfold, evaluate, adjust, and transform possibilities of my own life.

Religious experience is comprehensive and radical, and in this sense it is "totalitarian." It is the experience of the universe insofar as this is relevant for our most radical desiring. An experience is radical when it relates to my own life as an issue that is of ultimate concern to it; it is comprehensive when it encompasses and colors life's entire universe. Such an experience can only be taken seriously; it puts us in a serious mood.

My self-experience among persons and things can be modeled in many ways. Each way is an attempt to invent or discover a promising mode of relating to the universe. Religions and worldviews bear witness to the variety of these attempts; serious philosophies such as those of Plato, Aristotle, and the Stoics do the same in other, more conceptual ways. If experience is always a kind of experiment, this does not exclude periods of rest and consolidation. It is typical for religion, though, that none of the experimental stages into which it develops is experienced as an absolute endpoint. The most advanced persons continue to be moved by an impulse that prompts them to seek further, even if they do not quite know where they are going—and yet they are vaguely aware of a certain orientation, which they "feel" or with which they are "in touch." Thus every experience is an experiment with yourself. You are not only testing your possibilities, but also the manner and the tenability of your very experience. You are able to do this (i.e., the *fact* of your experiment is explainable,

your self-testing is possible) because there is something *in* you that
points beyond the encompassing experience that you are going
through here and now: a drive or desire that points toward "the
sought."

The fundamental experience at the heart of religion is thus: 1)
comprehensive, an experience of the whole of reality insofar as it
pertains to the experiencing subject; 2) *radical,* as an experience of
ultimate meaning; and 3) *dynamic;* not a static "state," but caught
up in an ongoing movement that is oriented by a primary force.

Is this perspective overly nostalgic or romantic? It might be, if
"the sought" were not as elusive as familiar, and if our seeking
were not a manner of discovering and assenting to the actual
reality of the here and now. Whether or not a radical "eroticism"
is a romantic idea can be discovered only by a self-critical experiment with that which attracts the seeker's love. If we refrain from
identifying "the sought" with any particular content or form of
human life, desire, by pushing us beyond the limits of particularity, will make us more realistic and more seriously profound.

A History of Desire

A philosophy of radical desire is a philosophy of the steps or
stages through which an experiencing subject must go to
approach the desirable. If we are able to indicate which stages are
necessary in order to approach Meaning and Presence, we can
answer the question whether the emphasis on experience
implies subjectivism. Intentions, dispositions, and preferences
that are bound to chance and spontaneous inclinations do not
lead into the radical dimension, but the desire that *constitutes* us
precedes all free designs and can thus be a norm. When it orients our experiments with a (more) satisfying way of inhabiting
the world, life becomes a history of seeking and finding—albeit
in a partial, preliminary, approximate, and fragmentary way—

what is ultimately important. To use an old expression, we could call this dynamism "the history of a soul."[5]

This is not to say that the history of desire's self-examinations should be a purely individual matter. The path of a soul's experience constitutes part of a broader history, which contains, for example, the history of the experiences of the family, the religious tradition, and the society to which the individual belongs. The experiment with life as a whole (and thus also with impending death) is a stake in both histories: the deepest dimension of both world history and an individual's history is the trial and error of a search that is achieved in an experiential and experimental way. This search for meaning not only dominates the history of religions, worldviews, and philosophies, but is also at the heart of art, morality, TV, and everyday concerns.

Experience and Thinking

The three characteristics given above as a preliminary description of fundamental experience make it necessary to confront experience with thinking. Surely philosophical thinking is likewise 1) comprehensive, 2) radical, and 3) a movement that propels itself ever onward.

A consideration of the relationship between thought and experience could begin with a preference for thought and accept as its guideline the well-known thesis that the criterion for establishing the truth of experiences is not to be found on the level of experience itself but in thought.

One way that thinking can address experience is by carefully controlling the inner coherence of the position implied in a specific form of experience. The formal inconsistency of certain assertions that express such experiences and the coherence (or lack of coherence) of the affections and practices characteristic for such a "position" invite reflection and logical analysis. A "logic" of the affections will often meet with conflicts and contradictions, but these do not yet justify a wholesale rejection of the experiential universe marked by them. Conflicts can be the expression of a crisis or transition that must be traversed. Since experience, as dynamic, travels along a path, it is to be expected that disharmonies and breaks lie along the way. They must be understood as emerging "between" or "in the middle of" different possibilities to which the subject feels attracted without having already decided which one to adopt.

If thinking presupposes not only formal competence but also the ability to evaluate the content and the mode of a specific way of life, from where does thinking then draw its criteria? If form and content cannot completely coincide, thinking must appeal to extralogical elements for the testing of our fundamental experiences.

An easy approach to religion investigates its radical, but vague and seemingly uncontrollable experiences from the perspective of trivial experiences that are much less problematic because they concern more superficial realities. Experiences that claim radicality, while contradicting the reality of our daily needs, are not only pretentious but illusory. The appeal to the givenness of cats, mats, ashtrays, colors and so forth functions as a negative criterion in excluding contradictory views and visions.

When we appeal to trivial experiences to disprove more profound experiences, we do not base our argument on any logic, but on the certainty of experiences that seem authentic and irrefutable to us. Something similar applies to the everyday experience of the ethical. The demand made on me when I meet another person confirms and restricts both my trivial and my cultural needs, and gives me (if I agree to it) another stance and disposition than the egoistic one. The normative experience that there are other persons with their own claims is an absolute condition for the rectitude of any experience that claims to be still more fundamental and comprehensive. The religious experience of a radical meaning which claims to lie at the heart of human existence cannot suppress the ethical experience. Moreover, since ethical experience is our awareness of an absolute command, it cannot be diminished by any other experience. Thus, a religion that requires us to ignore the command of absolute respect and dedication to others is necessarily false.

In this case, too, thinking does not appeal to a nonempirical content of its own but to an *originary experience* of a special kind. Religious experience is either fake or it is irreducible to any other sort of experience. For someone who has not had any experience of this kind (or has not yet recognized such an experience), it necessarily looks like a leap into the dark, but this dark is really full of a hidden light that can be experienced as such (i.e., as simultaneously hidden or dark and light).

Thinking has its own manner of experience;[6] it can be prepared and awakened by other experiences, but, like ethical, aesthetic or religious modes of experience, the experience of thinking is based on its own evidence. For thinking, too, begins with a leap, when it becomes aware of a radical desire for total reflection that cannot stop at systematic analyses and syntheses. Like the religious experience, it experiences many configurations without establishing any of them as final. Its dissatisfaction with the configurations it tries out emerges from a *still more fundamental experience* whose *clair-obscur* attracts us differently than any systematic totality. The desire from which thinking proceeds is similar to the desire that is expressed in the religions, but it is confined to a reflective and conceptual mode of contact with reality. Religion can be genuine without elaborate reflection, while philosophy cannot. Although reflection might seem a more developed and thorough form of radicalism, it cannot conquer the horizon of prayer and other religious phenomena. Notwithstanding its profundity, philosophy is therefore less radical and less risky, more distanced and cautious than genuine religion.

Philosophy and Theology

The foregoing has consequences for the relations between theology and philosophy. If theology is the reflective interpretation of a revelation whose content cannot be proved but only believed, and if philosophy, as autonomous thought, appeals only to universally shared experiences and a self-justifying logic, the difference between them seems to be fairly clear. Such definitions hide many difficulties and assumptions, however. For example, consider the following:

1) On what grounds can we believe anything that neither directly nor indirectly is based on experience?

2) What can be the significance and importance of a creed that cannot be experienced in any way? When people put it into words, it can be heard or read. But how can anyone appropriate its meaning, how can anyone agree to it "with heart and soul," if it cannot become an element of the experience through which the hearer is involved in the world and its history?

3) The contrast between belief and demonstration is much too simple. In all pursuits of truth there is an element of risk, and *all* basic positions in philosophy have something of a wager; they imply some sort of faith. Demonstrations unfold and clarify what we somehow already know; they can undo certain opinions or configurations of thought; but they cannot originate new original experiences.

4) The autarky of philosophical thinking is a modern myth. It betrays a particular mentality that is neither self-evident nor rationally justifiable. Modernity, too, has been an experiment with reality, an attempt to understand and treat everything as subordinate to the freedom of self-sufficient insights. However, even "enlightened" thinkers have come to the conclusion that independent thought is an illusion. Philosophy has changed into an interpretation of amazing adventures in perception, practice, life, love, guilt, mortality, and so forth.

If philosophy is a critical investigation of historical experiences that tests and transforms them into thought, the distinction between philosophy of the Christian religion and theology becomes problematic. How would a philosophical consideration of the Christian phenomenon differ from the theological reflection on the Christian religion in its historical factuality? When considering Christianity, philosophy and theology both focus on phenomenological description and insightful explication;

through finite human imagination and conceptuality, both try to understand what meaning(s) the phenomena of world and history according to the Christian perspective reveal. Both can be then seen as thoughtful elucidations of an ongoing history, skilled modes of reflection on the experiences of a religion that appeals to revelation without neglecting its social, historical and psychical phenomenality.

To what extent is belief in creation, incarnation, the trinity, and eschatology equivalent to the attitudes of gratitude, hope, adoration, joy, and peace that characterize genuine Christianity? The specific experiences of the historical movement in which Christian, non-Christian and anti-Christian elements have been intermingled can be interpreted as stages of one prolonged Experiment that has not yet come to an end—perhaps it has hardly begun. How are we to understand the various configurations of these elements? To what extent can Christianity be understood as a work of radical desire, and, at the same time, as an undeserved gift through which this desire receives an answer? What is the affective source of the Christian form of life?

A philosophy of radical desire should demonstrate how persons in individual and collective histories experiment with various possibilities of life. Each stage of their experimentation is a configuration in which visions, ideals, practices and emotions are woven together. A typology of these stages must bring to light their inner (in)consistencies and (dis)harmonies. In addition to a typology of stages, a philosophy of desire is a theory of human movement. It must declare why specific "figures of the spirit"[7] are deficient or only provisional. Internal conflicts and the inability to cope with the realities of life refute particular figures. When reality overpowers a familiar worldview, customary experiences are scattered and an old form of life and culture dies. The agonies occasioned by such disruptions can go on for a long time. A new basic experience presupposes the opening of a hidden source. A time of de(con)struction and confusion prepares the leap from which new forms can spring. Then these are again tested as to their viability. The description of a progress along diverse stages and its justification on the level of experience itself can draw from a wealth of itineraries, ladders and ascents that fill the spiritual traditions of the West, no less than those of the East.

The plausibility of historical manners of experience and the "necessity" of the shifts through which they change into other, equally historical manners have their own sort of rationality. A philosophy of desire is a hermeneutics of history as history of experimental dynamics. A great example here is Hegel's "science of the experience of consciousness."[8] But the specific manner of his project and the fundamental experiences of world, history, and God as they appear in it present a configuration that is dead. In great style, Hegel carried out the spiritual experiment that generates *and* summarizes the truth of the universe. Yet the dimensions of his project fell too short. Human desire reaches further, but it does not achieve completion. Hegel's "faith in Reason"[9] is a respectable summary of the manner in which the rational animal of modernity has attempted to situate itself in the universe. If we could read Hegel's system as a network of arguments that demonstrate the *plausibility* of its "totology,"[10] it would be a splendid experiment of the will to knowledge that tests how far it can go. Hegel himself saw it otherwise; witness his many assertions about the necessity of his deductions. It was not his desire for insight, but his claimed completion that caused the shortfall of his philosophy.

VII. WHAT IS PHILOSOPHY OF RELIGION?

The philosophy of religion, a pursuit analogous to the philosophy of nature, the philosophy of work, the philosophy of history or of mathematics, is the philosophical discipline that studies questions regarding the existence, the nature, the significance, the diversity, the function(s), the place, and the relations of religion. For an explanation of this sentence we must concentrate on the core concepts "philosophy" and "religion." Insofar as the design and method of the philosophy of religion correspond to those of other disciplines within philosophy, this is not the place to dwell on their similarity. As far as the characteristics that distinguish philosophy from other kinds of reflection are concerned, the first chapter has given a preliminary sketch and the other chapters have shown a specific style. I could declare that a good philosophy is not only phenomenological, but also dialectical, hermeneutic, logical, empirical, analytic, transcendental, and dialogical; however, all these epithets receive their proper meaning only within a metaphilosophical consideration

71

that shows their necessary coherence, and this is not the subject of this book.

Does the philosophical character of the philosophy of religion have its own special characteristics in addition to those it shares with other philosophical disciplines? This question is not meant as an empirical one, but as one that concerns the very design of this specific part of philosophy. The manner in which philosophers and theologians actually practice the philosophy of religion is less interesting than the question whether a philosophical reflection on the phenomenon of religion *by nature* implies a specific manner of thinking. If we develop philosophies devoted to nature, human beings, the state, morality, art, history, and religion, there is no reason to assume that the method we use in considering religion must be different from the one we practice in the other disciplines, unless religion, by its own nature, demands a different approach. Thus, the question posed above can only be answered by focusing our attention on the second central concept: the meaning of the word "religion."

In order to begin, the philosophy of religion must know what it is talking about. Thus, it must know what religion is. But at its beginning, it cannot know this in a philosophically justified way, since such knowledge (a philosophical insight into the true nature of religion and its relation to other realities) is precisely its goal (and hopefully its result). Here we encounter a common philosophical problem: in order to philosophize about "nature" or "work" or "history," we already have to know what nature, work, and history are. An even more fundamental problem is that to philosophize at all, we should already know what philosophizing is, but we can know this only at the end of a *meta*philosophy, which is a sort of "philosophy to the second power." To make a good (i.e., philosophically justified) beginning, philosophy must already be completed. This impossibility strikes us all the more sharply when we discover that, although we can strive and hope for such a completion, we cannot reach it. Thus a philosophical consideration of religion cannot begin with a philosophically justified definition of it. The beginning occurs as a tentative venture; although it can be adjusted and readjusted as our investigation proceeds, it cannot be dismissed completely because it remains a decisive part of our search. In some sense, philosophy of religion is nothing more than a series of attempts, each better (or worse) than the last, to give a good definition of what religion actually is. But this immediately poses the question: what grounds do we have for criticizing and changing a previous definition? What criterion will guide us in considering the real nature of religion? Where do we find such a criterion, if not in an adequate understanding of religion, which may be present and operative only implicitly and unconsciously?

Besides the general difficulty that accompanies the beginning of any philosophical inquiry, the philosophy of religion has its own special difficulty due to the nature of its subject matter. This difficulty lies in religion's claim to comprehensiveness: religion claims to be a comprehensive interpretation of reality. It encompasses the totality of human existence, the world, and history. This comprehensive (universal) character implies that philosophers cannot reflect on religion if they do not also intend to reflect on humanity, nature, culture, history, and the universe of all things and words. Although religion is not the only all-encompassing point of view, it imposes a specific *and* total perspective on philosophy. This makes it all the more difficult to begin: instead of one subject matter among others, philosophy of religion must consider the entire universe from the perspective of religion.

Where does the philosophy of religion get a preliminary and provisional definition of its subject matter? There is an answer that attempts to account for the difficulties indicated and yet holds to the philosophical origin of the concept of religion. According to this answer, the concept of religion is the result of other, preceding divisions of philosophy.

A *first* version of this answer is found in some forms of "philosophical theology," also known as "natural theology" (see chapter V). This discipline cannot be a philosophy of God in the same sense in which the philosophy of work and the philosophy of religion are considerations of empirical phenomena. For God, if anything, is not a phenomenon. Moreover, he or she or it is neither a subject among the other subjects about which we can reflect, nor the gathering or totality of all possible subjects. All these assertions rely on philosophical theology itself. In it, we cannot speak about God as an object given to reflection, but only as "something" thanks to which there are phenomena and thinking at all. From ancient times, "God" has been sought in philosophy as the *"Principle"* or *"Ground"* or *"Origin"* or *"Cause"* of all reality, a ground or origin that itself never comes to the fore; as *the One* that remains hidden, but upon which everything relies for its existence; as *the Truth* itself that makes knowledge and existence possible, etc. In our civilization, thinking has been practiced as grounding, and philosophical theology has presumed that there must be a final Why, which is what and how it is *because* it is that. Thinking about God is the most radical reflection on the universe; it cannot adequately be distinguished from metaphysics or general and special ontology.

If the arguments of philosophical theology are correct, humanity, the world, and history owe their existence to their relationship to God. Thus, at least an essential element (and perhaps even the core) of religion is shown by philosophy itself: the most fundamental relation between God and human reality is discovered by a grounding or "archaeological" thinking about finite and empirical realities in order to discover through them the *Archē* ((principle, beginning, origin, and ground) of all *archai*.

Three remarks on this answer seem appropriate:

1. If we defend the thesis that the relationship of human beings to God is the core of all religion, we must also explain how this relationship is latent in religions that do not believe in God, but only in gods, fate, or some other entity or force more or less analogous to God. If all religions are ultimately about the relationship of human beings to God, then philosophical theology does deal with the core of religion, *if* its "God" is the same as the God of religion.

Many scholars, especially theologians, have distinguished between "the God of the philosophers" and "the God of Abraham, Isaac, and Jacob" (i.e., the living God of the Judaeo-Christian tradition). It goes without saying that the concept of God that results from a philosophical reflection does not simply coincide with the God who lives in religious experience, preaching, or worship. Philosophical reflection attempts to say something in conceptual language about the God who is worshiped and celebrated, and it knows all too well that this "something" is very little. This awareness is evident, for example, in the strange statement that philosophy can discover *that* God is, but not *what* he is.[1] In the discussion about the relationship between the God of philosophy and the God of faith, the real question concerns how accurately a philosophy (e.g., that of Plato or Augustine or Descartes or Hegel) formulates something essential of the God who is confessed in religion, or, on the contrary, presents a caricature. In connection with the basic idea of Western philosophy as discussed earlier, we may ask: Is the God of religious experience recognizable (entirely or in part) in the absolute Ground of Western philosophy?

2. The arguments of philosophy (as ontology, metaphysics, or philosophical theology) about God are traditionally summarized in the so-called proofs for the existence of God. For a logic that we could call the "logic of the intellect,"[2] proofs are meaningful only when they connect finite realities with one Other. However, a conclusion that deals with an infinite ground of all reality can never follow from premises that contain merely finite terms. Philosophical theology, thus, relies (explicitly or implicitly) on a logic that allows the possibility (and, under certain conditions, the necessity) of making a transition from finite realities (or from the finite totality of all realities) to the nonfinite or infinite "Ground" of all finite reality. This transition (which for the logic of the intellect is an unjustified leap) is the common root of all the arguments about God in traditional metaphysics. The leaps through which we can think of an origin that does not originate from something else pose innumerable logical paradoxes for our

thinking. According to Hegel these can be overcome by Reason. Other philosophers deny this; they find every transgression of empirical finitude to be a sin against logic. However this may be, all proofs for God's existence begin from the conviction that there must be an ultimate ("last" or "first") ground, i.e., one that is radical and cannot be grounded any further, and thus is not relative, but absolute. Philosophical theology necessarily professes this conviction, since it practices thinking as a pursuit of the ultimate why. This conviction cannot be compellingly proved, certainly not by arguments available to the logic of the intellect, but this does not weaken its force. The "proofs" for God's existence are the expression of a radical mode of experiencing reality. The radicality of this thinking is a philosophical expression of the religious attitude. Its leap translates a fundamental attitude into conceptual language.

3. If the preceding is true, then philosophical theology seems to be a reflective endeavor that conceptually retrieves and, if successful, justifies basic elements of lived religion. Seen historically and psychologically, religion precedes philosophical theology. However, a philosopher attempts as much as possible to integrate conceptually what religion believes, claims, and does. Philosophy is the attempt to understand the how and the why of amazing phenomena, including religious phenomena, and their interconnections. Within philosophy, religious faith has no authority; in this sense, philosophy does not rely on religion, but its autonomous (re)construction of the relations between the universe and God grows out of the historical reality of religion. Philosophy of religion is the attempt to clarify the phenomenon of religion so that its reasonability comes to light.

This is also the definition of *Religionsphilosophie* that Hegel used, and with this we arrive at a *second* version of the answer mentioned above. For Hegel the universe is the self-realization of the Idea, while philosophy is the conceptual reconstruction of that same reality (nature, humanity, society, culture, and history). The essence of religion lies in the self-knowledge of the Idea, which, having concretized itself in nature and culture, celebrates its own being-for-itself in religion. The definition of religion is thus the result of all preceding definitions and conceptual developments. The philosophical elaboration of this definition is the conceptual translation of the full truth that is adhered to but not fully understood in religion. Hence philosophy is a higher form of spiritual self-knowledge than religion. For philosophy there are no final mysteries; it does not abolish religion, but understands its truth as necessarily belonging to the human universe.

The philosophical reflection on religion that is practiced in Hegel's system leads to a complete identity of the *content* of (the Christian) religion with the *content* of (the true) philosophy, although they present their content in different *forms*. Philosophy of religion coincides, in its content, with the whole of philosophy. The entire philosophical system is implicit in the true religion and vice versa; both contain the complete and absolute truth, but philosophy is needed in order to know this truth in its true form, understanding it while also understanding itself. The theoretical understanding of religion coincides with the endpoint of philosophy.

All this presupposes, however, that the basic truth of religion lay latent in philosophy from the beginning. The point of departure of Hegel's philosophy is a version of the basic axiom that was shown earlier to be the foundation of philosophical theology. It is most clearly expressed in the so-called ontological proof of God. If philosophy is the quest of the ultimate of all that is, this ultimate orients and directs and dominates all thinking from the outset. Hegel has only been more clear than other philosophers in exhibiting the reflexive and self-conscious character of the Ultimate and Absolute. The definition of the Absolute's self-knowledge in religion is an unfolding of the basic idea that governs Hegel's logic from beginning to end.

A *third* way to define religion by means of something else is reduction. From this perspective, religion is a façade or mask, an epiphenomenon or aura that has no truth of its own but vanishes like mist before the sun once we have seen through it. This is the way of Feuerbach, Marx, Nietzsche, and Freud. Psychopathology, psychoanalysis, sociology, linguistics, and other unmaskings of religious illusion share the approach of reducing religion to facts, experiences, drives, and so forth that the demystifyers deem less sublime but more real. Desire for God, religious experiences, and all "theologies" are illusory; the reality that lies underneath or behind them is hard and human or less than human. There are two possible ways to respond to such reductions. A philosopher who maintains the originality of religion can attack his reductionist opponents with their own weapons by giving a psychoanalysis of their psychoanalysis, an ideology critique of their critical assumptions, a sociological reduction of their sociological postulates. The starting-points of most reductions are vulnerable, since they themselves can be subjected to yet another meta-reduction. Only those whose starting-point consists in an irrefutable and originary experience of non-illusory, genuine evidence can resist a destruction of their starting point, but even that is not sufficient for a universal theory about all kinds of experience.

A second line of response consists in trying and testing the experiences from which the various reductions begin and comparing them with the experience that religion holds to be something primary and irreducible. What is at stake is not a massive rejection of every claim to demystification, but rather to find out whether religion, under certain conditions, "makes sense." Long before the "enlightened" critiques of Voltaire, Marx, or Freud, the great religions have had to contend with magic, superstition, and hypocrisy. The struggle of the Biblical prophets and the many ways of discernment and purification in all the spiritual traditions of East and West do not contradict the best observations, hypotheses, and theories of modern critique; both traditions must be retrieved in a constant search for greater authenticity. The real point of discussion is whether in and under all the perversion that often accompanies religion (just as it accompanies art and philosophy), we can still discover a pure and irreducible core, at least as a possibility yet to be realized. A positive answer to this question presupposes a pure experience of the religious, or (on the level of philosophy) a description and analysis of such a pure experience in contrast with forms of impurity that deform it under certain conditions. Such an answer coincides with the philosophy of religion if the latter aims not merely at a generalization of religious phenomena but at an understanding that would enable us to distinguish genuine and pure from inauthentic and false phenomena. To say it in traditional language, the philosophy of religion does not seek a lowest common denominator, but "the essence" of religion, its "idea," which (as Plato and others showed) is always at the same time an ideal.

The latter statements are not welcome in our positivistic climate. Many intellectuals think that the philosophy of religion—if it is possible at all—should begin with a definition of religion that is offered by the *science(s) of religion*. This opinion fits into a general theory of the relationship between philosophy and (positive) science according to which philosophy can be nothing else than a meta-scientific reflection on the results of the positive sciences. Science has its own criteria and methods which philosophy may not criticize but must simply accept. This is not the place for a general discussion of this standpoint and its less-extreme variations, but it is obvious that, by forcing philosophy into the position of an *ancilla scientiae,* such scientism can only be despised by those who are familiar with the philosophical tradition.

Any science cannot but begin its development with an unscientific concept of its subject matter (for example, language, society, religion or science): it draws on everyday linguistic usage, on current representations and prejudices, or on practices that are already going on. As science progresses, the original definition and theories are reformulated to accommodate new results and understandings. At any moment the current paradigms are only momentary results in a series of proposed theories that are constantly revised.

The method of modern science has its own ways of observation and selection; it omits much of the empirical data and emphasizes only certain of their aspects, for example, those that can be treated mathematically. Thus the concepts of religion that function in the contemporary sciences of religion are specific stylizations of religion as experienced by various believers. Being more comprehensive and more radical than positive science, philosophy refuses in principle to let itself be bound by a scientific framework. Without disregarding any of the positive findings of the sciences of religion, philosophy interprets them as attempts to clarify the religious phenomenon from limited perspectives; it must repeat for itself, from its own perspective and with its own methods, what the sciences do: reflect on *prescientific* experiences and ways in which religion is lived, perceived, stylized, and expressed. Philosophy accepts scientific points of view as particular and partial perspectives on the issue in question, but retains for itself the right to test these perspectives and to subordinate them to its own, wider and more radical perspective. If modern sciences had not turned away from philosophy and philosophy had not isolated itself, there would be no need for polemics about the competence of their approaches. A good science of religion cannot do without a good philosophy of religion, if only to know what religion "really is," but, on the other hand, philosophy of religion needs the sciences of religion, if it does not want to miss a wealth of concrete data and the various forms in which religion shows its nature or "essence."

In stressing the difference between philosophy and science, we should not give the impression that philosophy is less empirical[3] than the positive sciences. On the contrary, as a matter of principle, philosophy is more faithful and devoted to the empirical as it shows itself in a great variety of experiences. Philosophy tries hard not to be restricted by any single manner of experience or predetermined by any single schematism. Philosophers are aware that a completely "naked," purely immediate experience hardly occurs but rather presents itself as a core that is realized via many kinds of stylizations, especially imaginative and linguistic ones, but the idea of a core protects it against an absolutization of one-sided perspectives.

Both the science and the philosophy of religion must appeal to a prephilosophical and prescientific meaning of religion at work in experience and linguistic usage. At this point I will forego an analysis of *linguistic usage* as it relates to the religious, but I do want to remark on some problems concerning religious experience and its relation to the philosophy of religion.

An uncontaminated, naked experience of the religious is difficult to discover in the modern era. All our experiences, even religious ones, are marked by the scientific and philosophical culture in which we have been brought up. Perhaps there are moments in which some people forget everything else in an immediate relationship to God, but as soon as they speak about it, their story is marked by contemporary styles of interpretation. To be sure, there are believers who, in their religious language and experience, purposely disengage themselves from the experiential and hermeneutic patterns of the modern world, but such attempts, if they succeed, seem to condemn their religious experience to silence. Even "primitive" religions that have not yet come into contact with science and philosophy do not exhibit completely naked experiences of the essence of religion. Myths, kinship systems, taboos, and magical practices have already provided structures for their experience and models for any attempt to speak about them.

A philosophy of religious experience must confront the impossibility of separating religious experiences from the interpretations in which they are described. It must also confront the great diversity of such experiences: anxiety concerning magical powers, oceanic feelings of unification, gratitude to the Creator, nearness of the soul to the Beloved, grief over an all-permeating meaninglessness, and many other experiences seem to resist any attempt to bring them under one denominator. And how can we understand that many people seem not to have had any religious experience? How could they who once had them leave them behind in order to live a more sober and "realistic" existence? What is the meaning of all these differences that are already obvious on the level of experience?

A much-contested problem concerns the validity of interpretations suggested by specific experiences. Do assertions such as "I experience that God helps me" or "I experience that the world cannot exist on its own but relies on an infinite Ground" have the same epistemological status as "I see a table standing there"? Does the *experience* of religious realities give us sufficient warrant to make *assertions* about the existence and the nature of these realities? How must we ask and treat questions of experience, givenness, evidence, appearance, truth, and true assertions with regard to religion?

The most fundamental question for a philosophy of religious experience, however, is: what is meant here by "experience"? To what degree does religious experience coincide with experiences of other kinds, and to what degree does it differ from them? What is the relationship between religious interpretations and the experiential basis to which these refer? Who is capable of describing authentic experiences of the religious? How ought we go about a description that serves a philosophy of religion?

To begin with the last question, we can observe a religion from the outside as an interesting object for study, describing and analyzing its myths, tenets, and practices without committing ourselves to any personal response. A theory that expects truth from statements will treat religions as systems or collections of assertions. A person who is involved in religion, however, experiences religion as an engagement that is at once a manner of inhabiting the world, belonging with heart and soul to a community, finding an orientation in the universe, and meaningfully leading one's life. When we analyze the encompassing attitude that is typical of religious experience, we discover, "under" and "before" religious stories and assertions, a layer of personal experience that is characteristic for a specific style of existing. However, *through* religious texts and stories, prayers, poems, and theoretical assertions, even an outsider can get an idea of the experience that belongs to living religion. A sympathetic or empathetic experience is an indispensable element in the scientific or philosophical interpretation of any human phenomenon, all the more so of phenomena that touch upon the ultimate depth of human possibilities and aspirations. Behaviorist prejudices and wholesale

rejection of everything that looks like "introspection" have inca-
pacitated many scientists from doing justice to the most essential
experiences. They have thus deprived them of the right to be
called "empirical" in a true sense of the word. But what is the real
motive for the aversion to inwardness from which so many curi-
ous researchers suffer?

Ever since Parmenides, the epistemological status of experience
has been a great problem, and an overview of contemporary
schools and styles in philosophy could be given by presenting
them as different ways of dealing with the problem. A few remarks
on this problem with regard to religion have been offered in the
former chapter. Some additional hints will follow here.

Religious experiences are, on the one hand, related to empirical realities (a snowy landscape, for example, or the death of a
friend, the atrocities of war, the existence of the world, the procession of history), while on the other hand they are the experience of a reality (God, the gods, Moira, Spirit, etc.) that is neither
given immediately nor apart from those empirical realities, but
only "in" them. The reality of the divine is not some particular
invisible or spiritual reality among others, but the ultimate, to
which the human, cosmic, and historical universe refers, although
it is not part of it. The comprehensive and radical character of
this mystery requires that the experience in which it is felt,
desired, and lived be understood as likewise comprehensive and
radical. The "place" of this experience is the human "heart."
Thus, religious experiences are different from external or internal perceptions of less total and radical phenomena. This difference elucidates a number of difficulties that arise for those who
approach the problem of truth and evidence as a question of veri-
fying *assertions* about phenomena. I do not want to deny that the
domain of religion harbors far greater dangers of illusion than
are met within the perceptions of physical objects such as ashtrays and tables (which are also less fascinating); but this is not a
good reason for abandoning all religious phenomena to arbitrary
kinds of subjectivity. Subjectivity *always* plays an essential role;
the real question is not how to replace it by objectivity, but rather

how to distinguish purity, authenticity, and truthfulness from their false imitations. Tables (perhaps even ashtrays!) *can* be seen in a religious light; the issue is not so much *which* empirical data allow us to have access to the religious dimension; the mode of their appearances and our experience is much more relevant. Religious experiences of empirical phenomena run the risk of being obstructed by wishful fantasies or fanciful chimeras. As we have argued that among, "under," or "in" the many apparent experiences there is also the possibility of *genuine* and irreducible ones, we need to ask: what is the criterion for distinguishing the two? Whether certain experiences are genuine, originary, and irreducible can be decided only by the experiences themselves. In this respect religious experiences do not differ from experiences of the ethical or the aesthetic, or even from evaluative perceptions of flowers and human beings. Just as genuine perceptions can be distinguished from a *fata morgana* through specific procedures based on indisputable cases of genuine perception, so also the procedure for distinguishing genuine religious experiences from illusions (superstition, magic, etc.) is based on genuine religious experiences or genuine elements of mixed experiences and certainly *not* on experiences that have nothing to do with religion. To be sure, indisputable experiences of a nonreligious nature do function as negative conditions for the authenticity of religious experiences and assertions; also logical and ontological thinking, when it exposes absurdities and compares claimed experiences with the obvious or with grounded theories, can dispute or refute the authenticity of religious experiences and the validity of religious assertions. However, nothing other than *religious experience itself* is capable of carrying out a positive judgment and critique of its truth or illusoriness (just as there is no other criterion for the authenticity of other fundamental experiences, for example in the ethical and aesthetic dimensions, than the quality of such experiences themselves). This presupposes, however, that "religious experience" generally indicates a course of experience along many stages, whose degrees of authenticity and illusion correspond to different degrees of truth. Once engaged in this course the experiencing persons test and purify their own experiences and manners of experience in the light of a desire for purity. Far from denying the possibility that philosophical thought plays a role in the progressive purification of religious experience, these assertions emphasize the indispensable truth of prereflexive authenticity. To the extent in which thinking, as sympathetically engaged, is dedicated to unmasking inauthentic forms of experience, it is itself an element of the dynamic venture and adventure that we call experience.

Does this not introduce an extreme confusion? On the one hand, religious experience was upheld as a layer "under" or "before" its interpretations by myths, science, philosophical thinking, and so forth; on the other hand, thinking is now called an *element* of experience. It is typical for religious experience that it encompasses the entire person; not only the heart, but also the hands and the head. In this context "thinking" means primarily a reflective awareness of life as the most serious and comprehensive experiment with oneself. This awareness can adopt theoretical methods and techniques as elements of an ultimate or religious interpretation. Those who philosophize "with heart and soul" will never be able to isolate their existential self-awareness from what they question, seek, and know as philosophers.

The question remains, however, how reflection and other forms of thinking relate to other elements of experience such as imagination, belief, feeling, and disposition. Often the word "experience" is used, as distinct from "perception," "thought," and "imagination," to indicate the immediate aspects of experience, those that are hardly translatable into conceptual language: dispositions, feelings, emotions, and so on. It encompasses, then, the whole affective dimension of our engagement and the way of life that goes with it. The significance of such an experience depends on how we see the relation between affectivity and thinking. What does the ideal of rational justification, which philosophy has advocated from of old, imply for the fundamental value of feelings and inner experiences?

Here, too, we struggle with an expression of the dualistic prejudice of Western philosophy. A widely accepted position of our time subsumes all affective phenomena under the word "emotion" and rejects any claim to truth that resorts to "emotional language." This poses an absolute separation between rationality on the one side and arbitrary, uncontrollable subjectivity on the other. A more spiritualistic or idealistic version of this dualistic prejudice neither excludes the affective element of experience nor deems it unimportant, but sees it as a shadow of rational thought. Even here, feeling does not contribute to the discovery of truth, since it is but an obscure effect of the only light that enlightens humanity. Reason, and reason only, coincides in the end (and from the beginning) with God, while the affective order represents the animal or material element of pure darkness when it is left to itself.

A phenomenology of radical gratitude, hope, trust, delight, wonderment, and inner peace discovers their basic and irreplaceable significance when it understands them as modes of contact with the truth of reality. It need not prove that religious experiences in general are trustworthy; just like the experience of red or of a tree, the truth of a religious experience cannot be proved or disproved by anything other than a more attentive and more exact experience of *the same* sort. Religious experiences should neither be replaced by nonreligious experiences, nor by representations or conceptual structures, but we must show how impure experiences differ from pure ones and how a transition from the one type to the other is possible on the level of experience itself. For this we may appeal to the many itineraries in which the classics of Western and Eastern religion have described the progress of their "inner" life. However, a philosophy of religious experience is more than a repetition of experiential paths tried out by others; it tries to detect the illusions and the truths that emerge on those paths and to understand why human life is a journey.

The indispensability of prereflective religious experience for all truthful thinking about religion refers to a complete theory of the relationships between rationality, thinking, reflection, and affectivity. We may introduce such a theory by describing it as a version of Pascal's well-known aphorism: "The heart has reasons that reason does not know,"[4] an aphorism whose general sense, as well as the specific meanings, demands careful analysis and interpretation.

—//—

Now that we have delineated the philosophy of religion from prephilosophical experiences, religious science(s), and other disciplines of philosophy, there are still a few words to be said about the relations between the philosophy of religion and theology.

"Theology" is often practiced as a positive science of one religion. As such, it is no more than a synthesis of the empirical sciences that focus on this or that religion. In the West, theology is usually related to Christian belief, but scientific studies of Islam, Judaism, and Hinduism are just as possible, and such studies in fact exist. The scientific study of a religion does not in principle require that the scientists be adherents, but it is necessary that they immerse themselves in the spirit of that religion to the point where they appreciate the significance of the basic practices and beliefs within the context of its basic claims. From a psychological point of view, a believer is favorably disposed in this respect, but does he or she have sufficient distance to undertake a critical analysis?

A second meaning of "theology" consists in so-called "natural theology," which coincides with the philosophical theology discussed above. Its concern is to discover what human beings on their own can know about God, without appealing to any revelation or authority. The basis for this approach is the "natural" light of human reason.

A third meaning of "theology" appears when we reflect about the whole of a religion in order to discover its core elements, the coherence between them, and their significance for human life in the world, and thus to arrive at an insight into its way of life and interpretation. Such an investigation can be carried out by scholars who do not believe what they study, if they are able to imagine how participants in that religion feel, think, and behave. However, this cannot occur without some facility with philosophical methods and techniques, and thus usually not without a philosophical education (for which some theological schools allow too little space in their curriculum). This last form of theology coincides with a philosophy of religion directed toward a particular religion.

Christian theology, then, is the philosophy of Christianity. However, the word "theology" is most often used to combine a positive-scientific and a philosophical study of the Christian religion. It depends then on the style of the philosophy that is practiced in such a theology whether it also includes a philosophical or "natural" theology. Perhaps the ambiguity of the word "theology" has to do with the fact that many theologians still uphold the ideal of an integrated view of existence, in spite of postmodern fragmentation. However, philosophy too strives for a synoptic view; she too wants to be the "queen."

This ideal may encounter the resistance of an extra-scientific element, namely church politics: theologians (or philosophers) can, through their studies, come into conflict with the conceptions and practices that are holy to the church (or the movement or the party) to which they want to belong. When theologians or philosophers allow their practice of scholarship to be led by their community, they subordinate their thinking and experiencing to an authority whose relevance rests neither on scientific and philosophical grounds nor on subjective experiences, but on another claim or knowledge. Does this authority have at its disposal better, more authentic experiences or a better understanding of revealing words and traditions? If so, philosophers of religion cannot avoid asking what sort of nature and structure characterizes those experiences and insights and how they themselves should relate to the faith of that church.

VIII. Philosophy and Faith

A Christian who philosophizes cannot avoid the question of what philosophy has to do with confessing and living the Christian faith. In order to clarify this question before we even begin to seek an answer, we must give some consideration to the terms of the relationship between philosophy and faith. A complete analysis is probably not possible; even if it were possible, it could not take place at the beginning of a meditation of Christians about their way of life, since a full analysis would already presuppose a complete philosophy of faith and theology and a theology of philosophy. Our question accompanies the entire thought-life of any Christian philosopher who is serious about both the philosophical and the Christian aspects of his or her existence. The question must constantly be posed, clarified, and analyzed in new ways. This chapter is intended only as a preliminary consideration.

Metaphysics

It has become a commonplace to say that Western philosophers are the heirs of "the Greeks." Many qualifications are needed to safeguard such a statement from falsification. When we neglect the contributions of Roman, Arabic, and Germanic philosophers and identify "Greece" with the philosophical period of the Hellenic and Hellenistic world, we oversimplify our prehistory, and with it the memory on which our self-interpretation relies. It remains possible, however, to group a large portion of our philosophical heritage around the colossal figures of Plato and Aristotle. Whatever falls outside of this grouping is precisely that portion of our thinking in which the distinct vitality of Christian faith has been demonstrated through its concretization in Western culture. Reducing European philosophy to nothing but an elaboration of its Greek origin makes a brusque separation between philosophical thinking on one side and all other thinking, meditation, and contemplation on the other. Such a separation could explain why there are still philosophers for whom the history of philosophy dies with Plotinus or Proclus, only to be resurrected more than a thousand years later, with Bacon, Hobbes, or Descartes, from its medieval "degeneration."

An advantage of one-sidedness and exaggerations is that they help us create some order amid the turmoil of motifs that overtly or secretly dominate our thinking. For example, some of the particular contours of our own thinking are sharpened when we interpret it as a continuation of Platonic thought. Overwhelmed by the splendor of things, animals, stars, cities, and works that the world presents, thought can cut through their manifold to uncover the ever-present essences beyond all variations to see in them the unifying sources of all their variety. Once the *ousia* (essence) is discovered, observed, analyzed, and characterized, the world appears as a beautiful, well-formed, regulated whole. The vision of the essential "idea" sees also the *ideal* of those things; we encounter the essence's startling presence in their sensible appearance. Truth, goodness, and beauty lie in everything that shows itself as genuine and essential. The essence's or the idea's true reality, however, is not the origin itself; a mystery remains because the essence is given and displayed by "something" that, as pure radiance, is the ground of all those things that come to the fore in appearance. The vision that cuts through the phenomena to discover their essence cannot stop at a constellation of ideas, but reaches above and beyond toward the source of truth and being, which is blinding, yet irresistibly attractive. Since heaven, as anyone who has eyes can see, is the realm of radiant things, the orientation toward and beyond the truth of the essence leads "upward." Thinking is an ascent *(anabasis)* toward the good-and-beautiful itself, which grants all beings the splendor of their being. Such an ascent requires a conversion: without aversion from superficial appearances that lack consistency and light, our desire for truth cannot advance toward the real issues.

Christianity

If the allegation that all Western thinking is Greek is not contested, then we also may hold that all Western thinkers have been Christians. This second assertion no more means that all philosophers believe in the Gospel of Jesus than the first assertion holds that every philosopher endorses the thoughts of Parmenides or Plato. It does mean, however, that no single Western philosopher up to now has escaped the influence of historical Christianity. Even the atheists of our time bear traces of the religion that has profoundly marked our civilization, even if they seldom portray it adequately and even if historical Christianity is not a pure elaboration of the Gospel. Western atheism is a post-Christian atheism; it can combat the continuing actuality of Christianity, but it cannot eliminate its own Christian past. Neither Christianity nor atheism exists in an abstract form, elevated above culture and history. Modern and postmodern philosophy bear the distinguishing marks of Christian memory. In fact, after the failure of autonomous philosophy it is no longer so difficult to recognize within the work of all emancipated philosophers the traces of their prephilosophical past.

The radical and comprehensive significance of Christian faith implies, for Christians at least, that neither their thinking nor other activities will be able to avoid the inspiration of their faith. If that faith is genuine, their participation in the philosophical endeavor will bear the marks of a Christian way of engaging God, people, things, and the world. This way is concretized in specific conceptions with regard to God, the value of human life, the significance of death, and so forth, but it does not quite coincide with a specific system of dogmas or practices. More fundamental are the Christian moods of gratitude, hope, and compassion.

Christians who practice philosophy participate in the political and cultural structures of their time and place; they share social, symbolic, and theoretical frameworks with the non-Christian citizens of their nation. However, while their thoughts and expressions must be understandable to others, their deepest inspiration would be neither deep nor genuine if their practices and moods—even in the arts and philosophy—did not differ from those of the others.

The tension that results from that double participation can be observed in the early encounter of the Gospel with the Hellenistic and Roman world. The problem expressed in this tension has never been definitively solved, however. From the second century on, it has accompanied both the history of Christianity and the history of philosophy. After the modern experiment with autonomy, philosophers have once again recognized that the question of the relationship between faith and philosophy is a serious problem. Christians who are devoted to philosophy cannot skirt the issue, because it confronts them with the question of how they can combine two fundamental allegiances, both of which claim, in their own way, radicality and comprehensiveness.

Philo, Jesus' Alexandrian contemporary and fellow Jew, portrayed Plato as a student of Moses. As a scholar of his time, he considered Scripture to be a source for the eminent, though incomplete, learning of the Hellenes. Origen, Augustine, and many others followed his example, though they believed that the New Testament had fulfilled the promises made to Moses. Convinced that Jews and Greeks had become one in Christ, they used Greek wisdom to transform their Jewish heritage. They appropriated the Hellenistic and Roman culture as "spoils of the nations" in order to transform it into a wisdom of their own. Discussing with contemporaries both within and outside of Christianity and borrowing from everyone whatever they could integrate, they kept searching for adequate elucidations of the Gospel. From the outset, they assumed that the wisdom of faith was more than just another philosophy, but their belief in the Spirit of Pentecost also told them that the message of the Gospel could and should be translated into all languages, including those of Athens, Alexandria, Rome, and Milan. The interpretation of their faith demanded appropriate categories that would not restrict it to a particular vision bound to one culture only; yet, it was a "Greek" thought that offered them the material for such interpretations. No wonder that their use of that material was not always perfect and that it sometimes distorted the purity of their faith. Their problem is still ours: how can we think the kernel of faith, which is imperishable and eternal, through an appropriate use of existing philosophies, which belong to the cosmos that is passing away?

Platonism and Christianity

The temptation has always been great to identify the ascent of the mind described by Plato and his followers with the Christian journey toward God. The conversion *(metanoia)* that Jesus preaches as the condition for entering into the kingdom of God seems to resemble the inversion that Plato represents as the condition for the philosophical discovery of true reality. And how does the One that gives truth and being to all things relate to the God of Abraham, Isaac and Jacob, who is also the God of Jesus?

Early Christian thinkers have undeniably Platonized the Gospel, but they have also tried, both through and despite this hellenization, to transmit the universality of the Christian message. Substituting Jewish laws with pagan ideas would be a betrayal of the Gospel, if it were not emphasized at the same time that faith itself, the wisdom of God that sinners consider foolishness, transcends *every* particular form in which it may be incarnated. The philosophical thematization of genuine and central questions does not surpass a culturally and linguistically limited form of thinking and desiring with its own risks. Faith neither abolishes cultural incarnations nor absolutizes them, but it arouses time and again the most radical and most difficult questions for a thoughtful way of life.

The assimilation of (neo-)Platonic motifs by Christians whose faith does not extinguish their questioning but spurs them on to profound thinking has led to a great but ambiguous alliance of metaphysics with theology. Their relations have become a problem for all heirs of Luther and Barth, Nietzsche and Heidegger. The God of Plato, Aristotle, the Stoics, and the Neoplatonists, the unmoved Origin toward which everything strives via the noetic capabilities of the human soul, is partially identified with the God of history celebrated in the Jewish and Christian Scriptures. The relations between humans and God have been thematized with reference to a struggle between soul and body. The Platonic identification of the human being with the soul,[1] the opposition between "care for the soul" and concern for bodily gratification,[2] the contempt for the sensible and sensuality, and so forth, found a willing audience in most of the Church Fathers. Not only were these ideas "in the air," but they also seemed to harmonize with the Pauline opposition between spirit *(pneuma, spiritus)* and flesh *(sarx, caro)* and the Johannine opposition between "the world," which walks in darkness, and the spirit of truth, which is the one and only light. Good exegesis has taught us that these biblical oppositions have little to do with the dualisms of metaphysics, but rather characterize different attitudes with regard to God's work and word. For that matter, we may argue that Plato himself had primarily ethical concerns in mind when he contrasted such "somatic" interests as eating and sex, idle chatter and injustice to the purified way of life of someone who is in love with beauty, goodness and truth. The ambiguity of these thoughts continues to play a large role today, notwithstanding faith's repeated assurances that everything created, as a gift of grace, is good or even very good. Western Christianity is still not completely free from its suspicion of the body, and there is still a strong tendency to conceive of the resurrection as a continuation or revival of a disembodied soul.

This Platonizing tendency is clearly evident in the writings of the most influential modern philosophers from Descartes through Hegel. The latter's apotheosis of Western spiritualism unfolds the reality as a Spirit that produces its opposite as a shadow of itself, in interaction with which it hierarchically brings forth its self-incarnations. Hegel's spiritualism can be understood as a translation of humanity's desire to be its own cause (or "source" or "father"). Whoever thinks rules.

Do the traditional conceptions of spirit and body, masculinity and femininity, sexuality and reproduction, authority and obedience result from pagan motifs or rather from Judeo-Christian sources? Even if a predominantly pagan inspiration could be demonstrated, the real question is whether Christianity has not followed a double track. While, on the one hand, engaging in a non-Christian culture, it has, on the other hand, transmitted, both through and in spite of this particularism, the inspiration of faith, though not untouched by impurity. Is this mixture the way a faithful community that is "simultaneously just and sinner" gives an historical shape to its love for the Truth?

Prayer and Reflection

The post-Christian culture that has prevailed in the West for the last century resembles in some aspects the pre-Christian culture of the Roman Empire; it confronts thinking Christians with comparable questions. However, our modernity differs from the ancient world through the formalistic universality of its utilitarianism and the obsession with freedom of its intellectual elite. We want to understand the universe in order to possess and rule it for the "good of all." The emergence of the modern project was a reorientation of our attitude to reality; it generated a new relationship between philosophy, existence, and faith. In the Platonic tradition, contemplation of the ideas was an integral element of the ascent to the One Good itself. The Christian thinkers recognized in this an affinity with the believer's looking up toward the one true God; the Greek idea of *anabasis* was thus incorporated into their theory of contemplation as an exodus. Understanding "the One" and "the Good" as pseudonyms for the God of Abraham and Jesus, they tried to unite their reflection with their adoration in a unified dynamic of their lives. Many of their best texts originated within the framework of their liturgical celebrations, when they thoughtfully expounded what Christians confess as the ground of their gratitude and hope; but many of their scholarly texts, too, written in contemplative solitude, are marked by prayer. Thus Pseudo-Dionysius begins his work on *Mystical Theology* with a vocative ("O Trinity"), followed by the prayerful invocation of God's incomprehensible but adorable attributes, which are then reflectively elucidated in an address to "Timotheos" (i.e., all "Godfearing" readers).[3] The prayerful exordia of Augustine's *Soliloquies* and his *Confessions* give witness to the compelling force that gives his recollections their deepest meaning. In Anselm's *Proslogion,* prayer and thought alternate throughout, and the reader who ignores their unity cannot understand the text.[4] Bonaventure's *Itinerarium mentis in Deum* is framed by worship and supplication, and the whole text is borne along by a silent *cantus firmus* that unifies its thoughts and feelings. All these and many other texts testify to the double path those authors followed. Their reflection is inspired by a desire for God. Thus they make it known (in formulations that recall Platonic motifs) that the ultimate goal of all knowledge is not comprehension, but a mental "excess" *(excessus mentis)* that cannot be acquired but only received. That all investigation ultimately points toward a creative generosity presupposing not possession, but receptivity, is expressed toward the end of Bonaventure's *Itinerarium,* when he quotes the aforementioned prayer of Pseudo-Dionysius in connection with such an excess:

O Trinity beyond essence, beyond God, beyond-best Guardian of the Christians' wisdom of God, direct us to the supremely unknown, superluminous, and most sublime summit of mystical words. Bring us there, where new, absolute, unchangeable mysteries of theology are shrouded in the superluminous darkness of a silence that teaches secretly in the deepest dark surpassing all manifestation and resplendent above all splendor, while bringing everything to light—a darkness which fills invisible intellects with an over-flowing abundance of splendors of invisible goodness above all good.

In the blinding light of this prayer, Bonaventure can then also, at the end of his ascent, quote the following from Dionysius' text as a methodological instruction for the disciple-thinker:

And you, my friend, hold fast on the good way, if you want to gain sight of the mystery. Let all senses and intellectual activities, all sensory and invisible things, everything that is not and everything that is, fall behind you, and let yourself, as much as possible, in ignorance be brought back to the unity with Him who is above all being and knowledge. Through the immeasurable and absolute excess of a pure mind beyond yourself and all beings, rise up toward the super-essential radiance of God's darkness[5]

Christianity and Modern Philosophy

The turn that thinking has taken in the modern age is expressed in the dominant role of self-reflection, in the strong sense of the word: all thinking turns the thinker back on himself, since self-consciousness has become the space within which all being and truth must be found. Descartes' elucidation of consciousness as the only possible and in principle comprehensive reality is symptomatic of the closedness within which the self-declared autonomous I secures and celebrates its liberation from everything that is not I. The only authority acknowledged is that of self-evident representations, present within the interiority of the self-sufficient *Cogito:* but the development of modern thought shows in various ways that it cannot succeed in reaching complete independence.

Since thinking has turned into consciousness' reflection on itself, the upward look toward a "super-essential" Absolute no longer plays an essential role in the concrete process of thinking. Nevertheless, at the end of Descartes' third *Meditation,* the God who is worshiped in Christian faith appears once more on the stage. After the arguments in which the "idea" of a perfect being is investigated with regard to his existence, Descartes decides to dwell on the wonder of this completely perfect God, devoting himself in all quietness to the contemplation of his attributes, and "to admire and adore the incomparable beauty of this immense light, at least so far as the power of my spirit, which somehow remains blinded by it, will permit me."

As a believer, Descartes knows that philosophy and science are not sufficient to fill a human life with meaning: "As faith teaches us that the sovereign bliss of the life beyond lies only in the contemplation of the divine Majesty, so we experience now already that a similar—be it incomparably less perfect—contemplation lets us enjoy the greatest contentment which we can experience in this life."[6]

In this passage Descartes utters no prayer, though he certainly points toward an adorable God who transcends all thematization. The function of this passage, however, is ambiguous. It does connect Descartes' metaphysical argumentation with the most important question of a human life, which cannot be answered by philosophy and science alone. Within his rigorous theory, however, there is no place for the kind of contemplation indicated here. Descartes makes this clear on several occasions, for example, in his *Discourse on Method* and in the letter dedicating his *Meditations* to the theologians of the Sorbonne,[7] where he sharply delineates his metaphysical considerations from faith, which he otherwise wants to respect completely.

Descartes' separation of faith from philosophy and science, equally upheld by many of his contemporaries, was a great disaster for the thinking of Christians in the modern age. Not only has theology fallen into a miserable sort of reflection; the philosophy of Christians, as well, has assumed the form of a systematics in which the experience and the meaning of a lived life hardly find a place. For non-Christians, philosophy could take root in what remained of Christianity or in other, non-Christian convictions, but for them, too, a sustained (and not only provisional or merely methodological) separation between fundamental convictions and experiences on the one side and scientific philosophy on the other side turned the "love of wisdom" into a barren and boring activity. The ambivalence of Descartes appears most clearly when he writes (for example, in the prefatory letter to the French edition of *The Principles of Philosophy*)[8] that the meaning of philosophy and science consists in its service to the time-honored ideal of wisdom, which combines knowledge with good conduct and happiness, while, on the other hand, treating the Christian life as a separate domain that lies outside the path of science. More radical thinkers such as Spinoza and Hegel could not abide with such ambivalence. Betting on autonomous thinking, they subjected the dogmatics of believers to pure reason and translated the dogmas of faith into rational insights. Thus originated the modern gnosis of a theory that absorbed faith by cleansing it from all that goes beyond comprehensibility. Much of the remaining history of philosophy can be understood as a sustained reduction of the theological elements still lingering in the systems of early modernity.

Actually, modern metaphysics continued the Greek and European traditions of depreciating nature, the body, and sensuality, and even sharpened this depreciation. Descartes' aversion to the senses provides the classic example, unequaled in the history of philosophy, of an epistemological and metaphysical duality. Though not certain how the substances which he called "soul" and "body" could constitute a single person, he did not perceive the inner contradiction of his approach. He was fully and willfully aware, however, of his ruthless identification of human beings with their consciousness, which he conceived as "a thinking thing" and identified with what was previously called soul *(anima)* and spirit *(spiritus).* In order to isolate the domain of (self-)consciousness, he cut it off from faith and its accompanying traditions, the community in which faith was practiced, and the prevailing morality (which was also his own, even if he accepted it only provisionally). He even separated it from corporeality and the whole of material nature, thus necessarily depriving nature and the body of their inspiration and symbolic power. Metaphysics was narrowed to the reflective analysis of a self-conscious interiority filled with representations, assured by God. As nonincarnated spirits isolated from faith, human beings came to stand above the world in the position of rulers who oversaw the earth, possessed it, and exploited it according to their own pleasure. God's relationship with the world has been reduced to a guarantee for the certainty of secular knowledge; it is no longer known in the form of a radiant glory that shines in all things. The world has become prosaic, reduced to something useful for our needs. As "master and possessor of nature,"[9] man can still appeal to God and faith as ultimate foundation, but they remain confined to an invisible and inoperative background. If we recall the (neo-)Platonic vision, we see that the upward striving dynamizing all phenomena and ideas has been replaced by a mechanistic system in which there is no place for a higher goal or a highest Good. The goal is a complete mastery that scientifically controls the world and history. As far as the royal road of science is concerned, prayer and the upward gaze have become marginal, naïve, and infantile. Scientific philosophy takes pride in its independence from all traditions; it is sufficient to itself. Faith and history, gratitude and hope remain outside the project of appropriation and self-possession. The mysteries of human existence are changed into problems to be solved by methodical rigor. It goes without saying that in these circumstances, faith degenerates or disappears. It is also true, although perhaps less evident, that Christians who adopt the ideal of an autonomous philosophy condemn their faith to irrelevance.

Faith and Thinking Now

The dream of an autonomous philosophy has reached a dead-end. Not a single philosophy of the twentieth century still holds on to the illusion of a philosophical system without fundamental assumptions and prejudices—which, since they are fundamental, cannot be justified. This disillusionment does not imply that the project of modern autonomy has been worthless. It has at least taught us what strict requirements accompany the desire for a justification that is as rigorous as possible. We must also grant the requirement that we make our own postulates as explicit as possible when we want to take "the others" seriously.

It has become a generally accepted point of departure that our living and thinking are rooted in the soil of unconscious and unprovable assumptions, traditions, and customs. This is one of the characteristics that seems to distinguish the current situation from the modern ideal.[10] The hope that a perfectly autonomous philosophy would be possible has been given up, although it still permeates the average introductions to philosophy. If faith is an unprovable but meaningful and certain presupposition, it seems impossible for a self-conscious and enlightened Christian thinker to ignore this presupposition in his thinking. *Is* faith, however, a presupposition (or a complex of presuppositions) in the same way in which fundamental postulates of philosophy are?

Many Christians have represented their faith as a monolithic and unchanging whole, but philosophical and theological analysis can discover in it all kinds of temporally and culturally determined elements of an economic, political, financial, diplomatic, juridical, theoretical, moral, and religious nature. Thus many traditions of Christianity have included Jewish, Roman, feudal, monarchical, nationalistic, and bourgeois-liberal particularities. Insofar as faith has been concretized in the pattern of a specific culture or time (and without such a concretization, faith would not be genuine) it is just as transitory as that pattern; and a community of faith, like any society, finds great difficulty in the transition from a familiar ethos to new forms of life that are initially experimental and clumsy. Thus it travels through a sort of no-man's-land during times of transition—with all the disorder and struggle that accompany it. As the historical form of faith assumed at a specific time and culture comes under the ground-breaking criticism of a new time, people of faith are faced with the difficult question how to experience and express the Gospel anew. Although Christianity in its beginning was dynamic enough to break through the frameworks of the existing Judaism, in the course of history it has become identified in many ways with other frameworks that threatened to turn it into superstition and idolatry.

One can, for example, protest against the identification of faith with autocratic power structures by pleading for a reincar-nation of the Gospel in democratic structures more appropriate to the twentieth century. In the struggle that arises from this con-frontation both sides can make the mistake of seeking salvation itself in one political pattern or the other. Twentieth-century people cannot think in the terms of feudalism or absolute monarchy; but it still does not follow that the gospel prescribes democratic behavior. If the gospel is to be realized within our cultural framework, it must be concretized in juridical, political, moral, aesthetic, communicative, and liturgical patterns appro-priate to the vital possibilities of our society—unless, of course, these patterns are aberrations. The patterns of Western civiliza-tion in the twentieth century include the principles of democ-racy, the basic rights of all people, the political, juridical, and moral equality of man and woman, universal participation in the exercise of power, and so forth. When present-day Christians understand their time and do not superstitiously insist on histor-ical instantiations as *non plus ultra,* they practice common demo-cratic procedures. However, it would be a mistake to identify the Gospel and faith with the ideals of democracy or other political systems, such as socialism, the antinuclear movement, environ-mentalism, and so forth. As justified as these movements may be, they are only timely attempts to do justice to the human and nat-ural reality.

Like politics and morality, philosophy is a dimension of Western existence in which Christian faith must be incarnated. This dimension also cannot be concretized as a *philosophia perennis*, but only as the specific manifestation of a transitory culture. Just like the philosophies of the Hellenistic era and the Middle Ages, the modern project of an autonomous philosophy, with the spiritual climate it produced, is a particular elaboration of the thinking that we cannot avoid ever since it was begun by Parmenides and Heraclitus. The current situation of philosophy differs considerably, however, from the one that was dominant up to the beginning of the Christian era. Some try to express this difference through epithets such as "post-Christian" and "postmodern," but it is difficult to find a positive term because there seems to be little coherence and convergence between the disparate positions into which philosophy has split. In any case, we cannot look to faith as a panacea to solve philosophical problems. Philosophers will have to make their way with their own tools through the tangle of conflicting positions and tendencies. The methodological abstractions implicit in the practice of philosophy, however, cannot prevent a philosopher from giving an account of the orientation of his or her life—at least to himself or herself. A philosopher who also believes—or a believer who also reflects—cannot avoid a thoughtful thematization of the connections that link participation in the traditions of faith to participation in the history of thought. Such a thematization is at home in the philosophical project of fundamental justification, but it is also an essential part of theology. A certain naïveté is good, but whoever has experienced how impassioned reflection can be cannot stop thinking until the radical unity of philosophy and theology has become an issue. The thought of a well-trained philosopher who thinks and believes authentically does not exclude the radical meaning of faith from the dimension of thought. Blondel, Marcel, Guardini, Weil, Rosenzweig and Levinas are examples of this sort of thinking. In contrast, the attempt to eliminate religious faith when engaged with philosophy is an unfruitful strategy. Although methodological abstractions are

necessary in order to guarantee the purity of rational argumentation, the method itself demands that we show how all abstractions
fit into and are integrated in the human actuality of life, thought,
and action in the real world. By pitting faith and philosophy over
against each other, we become aware of the relative independence of both, but this does not exclude the awareness that they
are necessarily and radically intertwined. Abstractions, distinctions, and analyses must be integrated in a more concrete thought
that understands their unity.

After the celebratory clamor over the modern emancipation
to self-enlightened autonomy has subsided, it is once again possible for thinking to come close to life as it is fundamentally experienced and actually lived.

"What is it, then, which has made the souls forget their father,
God, and be ignorant of themselves and him, even though they
are parts which come from his higher world and altogether
belong to it? The beginning of evil for them was audacity and
coming to birth and the first otherness and the wishing to belong
to themselves. Since they were clearly delighted with their own
independence, and made great use of self-movement, running
the opposite course and getting as far away as possible, they were
ignorant even that they themselves came from that world; just as
children who are immediately torn from their parents and
brought up far away do not know who they themselves or their
parents are."[11]

"Though they knew God, they did not honor him as God or
give thanks to him, but they became futile in their thinking, and
their senseless minds were darkened. Claiming to be wise, they
became fools...."[12]

"The spirit searches everything, even the depths of God. For
what human being knows what is truly human except the human
spirit that is within? So also no one comprehends what is truly
God's except the Spirit of God."[13]

IX. THE PROBLEM OF CHRISTIAN PHILOSOPHY

History, sociology and cultural anthropology have turned the earth into a museum of cultures. Similarly, the history of philosophy is in danger of transforming its ongoing search for truth into a museum of philosophies, where none are taken very seriously, although some may be deemed interesting enough to be studied with admiration and a kind of detached sympathy. A museum displays many specimens without imposing specific preferences on its visitors. Besides modern, postmodern, classical and medieval philosophy we now also have Continental, American, French, German, African, feminist, analytic, phenomenological, Jewish, and perhaps even Christian philosophy. Some contemporary professionals of philosophy claim that philosophy is essentially Greek; others admit the possibility of a Jewish, Greek-Jew or Jew-Greek, philosophy, but "Christian philosophy" is mostly seen as a hybrid. Even for Christians who are devoted to philosophy, it is a problematic term. There is a strong suspicion that to be a Christian and to be passionately engaged in philosophy are mutually exclusive. Isn't the separation of faith and philosophy one of the most legitimate and well-probed axioms that belong to the legacy of modernity?

On the other hand, it does seem odd that Christians who are engaged in philosophy express a greater affinity toward those modern and postmodern thinkers whose commerce with truth seems to be un- or anti-Christian than toward the tradition that extends from Clement to Blondel and Marcel, thinkers who did not hide their attachment to the Christian community. Must philosophy be restricted to questions that are not of ultimate importance? Is philosophy a skill or science like other skills or sciences, or does it involve us in questions of life and death, of nihilism and ultimate meaning? Today it has again become possible to treat the question of Christian philosophy seriously, and we are invited to retrieve a long tradition of Christian thought in a postmodern or post-postmodern way. This enterprise involves the invention of a new relation to modernity and to its axioms about the nature of philosophy.

In this chapter I will focus on some thematic aspects of our problem by concentrating on the following three questions:

    I. What is philosophy and how do we engage in it?
   II. What should we understand by the word "Christian"?
  III. How are the philosophical and the Christian moments connected in a person who is both a Christian and a philosopher?

The perspective from which I will reflect on these questions is that of one who attempts to be a Catholic and a philosopher at the same time. I am aware that these questions have been debated before, particularly in France sixty years ago, but the situation has changed profoundly since the heyday of neo-Thomism. Neoscholasticism has disappeared; exegesis and history have shown how many meanings the word "Christian" has; the modern idea of an autonomous philosophy has made room for conceptions according to which philosophy is always rooted in prephilosophical soil and fed by nonphilosophical moods, mores and traditions. We must therefore redefine the terms of our problem and start from the historical information and the thematic styles of thought that are available today, an enormous task to which I can offer only a modest contribution.

I. Philosophy

The contemporary situation of philosophy cannot be understood without a thorough knowledge of modern philosophy, by which I mean those methods and doctrines developed in the period from Hobbes and Descartes to Hegel and 20th-century analytic and scientific philosophy. All postmodern philosophies from Feuerbach, Marx and Nietzsche, to Heidegger, Levinas and Derrida are parasitic on modern predecessors whom they try to overcome in various critical ways. Most contemporary philosophers know little about the more than two thousand years of thinking that separate modern times from Plato and Aristotle. Nonetheless, they deem their acquaintance with the last 400 years of thought to be a sufficient basis from which to understand *the* history of philosophy. Fortunately, a host of historical studies have made it impossible to identify philosophy with postmedieval thought. It has become a symptom of ignorance to see antiquity and the Middle Ages as a mere preparation for the scientific projects of our own time. Let us distance ourselves from such crude assumptions and challenge the monopoly of a certain "enlightenment" in setting the stage for philosophizing and the understanding of our history. With a view to the problem of Christian philosophy, at least the following modern assumptions must be made explicit and, perhaps, rejected:

1. The modern subject-object schema is determinative for all rigorous thought;
2. Philosophy is synonymous with theory;
3. Philosophy is fundamental and autonomous; as such, it must be clearly separated from any other form of thought and language, such as literature, religion, theology, and spirituality.

A full explanation of these assumptions and their consequences cannot be given here, but since it is crucial to see their importance to our problem and to question their solidity, I must at least briefly summarize the extent to which they have been overcome after a hundred years of phenomenology.

Subject-Object

Phenomenology has shown that neither human experience nor being can be understood within the framework of a subject in confrontation with objects. Objectivity is a specific kind of phenomenality; there are many other, and more primordial, modes of being. Since the phenomenality of being, as that which we feel, smell, desire, enjoy, recall, and so forth, each time demands an appropriate response, we cannot characterize the human openness to phenomena as the consciousness of a subject, if "subjectivity" is understood as a correlate of the phenomena's objectivity. Appearance and openness form a much vaguer, freer and wider horizon than the narrow, but scientifically more manageable one of the subject-object correlation. The vagueness of the wider horizon invites us to investigate all the possible modes and ways of being, and to explore the entire variety of beingness and perception characteristic of the human universe as such. Husserl, Heidegger, Scheler, Marcel, Merleau-Ponty, Levinas, Ricoeur and others have laid much of the groundwork for a new era in philosophy. They have radically transformed the soil of philosophy, thus altering the possible uses of philosophy in science or theology.

Not only has the analogy of being again become a central issue for thought, but the givenness of beings in their various modes of being has been discovered—or rediscovered. By making us aware of the ontological difference between Being and beings, Heidegger awakened us to new amazement about the emergence of beings in their being given as such. That there is being at all is the wonder of wonders. The givenness of being in all its diversity is that which most amazes thought and urges it to unfold its questions.

Theory

Modern philosophy is theoretical. *Theoria* was also the ideal for Plato and Aristotle, and even for Thomas Aquinas, who saw perfect theory as the happy fulfillment of our most radical desire; but modern theory has a different character. Its relation to reality, including the objectivity of the outer world and the interiority of human consciousness, is characterized by the search for objective knowledge of the subject's objects, and its own nonsubjectivistic, universally valid and thus "objective" subjectivity. The theoretical intention does not coincide with the objective or objectifying one, however; theory is wider and permits other forms of being acquainted or being in touch with things. It encompasses many ways of understanding; even the acquaintance with being as such has been thematized as a mainly theoretical—meditative, questioning or contemplative—way of dealing with our being-in-the-world.

Modern theory typically maintains a distance from emotional and practical involvement. It relies on observation and intellect, but is suspicious of emotion and delays praxis (and ethics as the theory of human praxis) until later, when theory is complete. The only exercise it deems necessary is experimental and logical: accurate perception, analysis and reasoning seem to be the only tools needed for the discovery of nonsubjectivistic, scientific truth. Very different from the Eastern and Western traditions of spirituality, the practice of modern science and philosophy demands no emotional or behavioral preparation; the quality of a human life is irrelevant to theoretical truth and validity. The modern idea of an introduction to philosophy does not involve an ethical preparation of mind and body; without any *psychagogia* the teacher starts directly from the pupil's intelligence and extant knowledge, in order to show how this starting point must unfold into deeper and more complex thoughts. Truth is a set of true sentences or theorems—ideally the totality of all theoretical truths; it can be known indiscriminately by saints and criminals. The only conditions for good philosophy are loyalty to the facts,

which are obvious to everyone whose perception is not handicapped, and "faith in reason."[1]

Phenomenology and the human sciences have demystified the
mastery of theoretical reason by disclosing its entanglement in
the emotional and practical life of individual thinkers, communities and cultures. Historical studies have revealed how much of
Descartes', Spinoza's, Kant's and Hegel's ideas are rooted in, suggested by, and even dependent on unproven emotional attachments to certain points of view.[2] Their search for happiness or
salvation committed them to positions founded on emotions as
well as the intellect. Thematic studies, first among them being
Heidegger's *Sein und Zeit,* have shown how thinking, in the narrow modern sense of theoretical investigation, is rooted, embed-
ded, oriented, guided, tuned and enveloped by something much
deeper: an acquaintance with world, things, and events which lies
before or under the differentiation of theory. This acquaintance
is neither objective nor subjective,[3] because it is much more radical than such a superficial distinction. The appropriate human
response to most phenomena and modes of surprising, touch-
ing, impressing or affecting is affection rather than observation
or intellectual grasping. As being in time, this affective acquaintance is not a static fundament or a treasure, once-and-for-all
acquired or acquirable; it is not a set of principles or a toolbox
for disclosure. It is desire, drivenness, movement, motion: a passionate involvement that tries to cope with the world, with
others, and with the riddles of life itself.

This passion has a history: a history of responding and experimentation. Human life is touched, moved, affected by phenomena which invite appropriate responses. Life itself demands a
responsive and responsible self to live it in an appropriate—i.e.,
authentic, correctly corresponding—way. This demand cannot be
fulfilled without the trial and error of the self's adjustments to its
life-filling task. The experiment of life is the ongoing practice of
the self's responsive attempts to cope with the reality of its being
on earth. Experience, *empeiria,* is the general name for all the
modes of being involved in affections and affective responses by

which the self is constantly transformed. If its orientation is good—which presupposes a turn from inauthenticity to authentic responsivity—the transformation makes the self better and wiser. This enables us to feel, behave, and speak accurately in response to the phenomena of life and world. Speaking to or about them must do justice to their appearance and touch them in what they truly are, even if they blind or paralyze the self's experience.

Modern philosophy and science have developed a deep mistrust of such personal involvement. Both warn that the universal validity of the truth should be protected by unemotional objectivity. The subjectivism of emotions and the particularity of individual experience must be corrected by critically distant observation and cold rationality. The correction of the self's modes of coping with reality was sought in an "emendation of the intellect,"[4] not primarily in an adjustment of affective responsibility. Emotional adjustment was seen as a result of conceptual considerations; these could and should dominate and rule the chaotic and irrational mass of unguided pleasures, drives and inclinations.

The modern exclusion of affectivity from the basic orientation of a life in search of wisdom devalued all those phenomena which cannot be perceived and do not exist unless we accept them as surprising, amazing, moving, wonderful, delightful, happy, terrible, horrible, and so on. Philosophy was thus robbed of all passionate, fascinating, admirable or simply interesting experiences. Even boredom, the inevitable result of this sort of rationalism and empiricism, was not allowed to have a say in philosophy. Passions and emotions do not allow us to exclude them from philosophy, however. It is therefore quite possible to write a history of the unrecognized passions revealed in the systems of Descartes, Spinoza, Leibniz, Kant, etc. Notwithstanding their efforts at objectification and scientification, the texts of these philosophers are still interesting because of the passion that drives them. A fundamental mistake of the modern project is its illusion that passions and emotions can be civilized by anything other than a passionate and emotional purification of these same passions and emotions. The appropriate responses suggested and demanded by a beautiful tree, radiant eyes, a deep depression or similar phenomena are essentially emotional; they cannot be replaced by "objective" observation or theory. Involvement is an unavoidable part of the suggested response. Respect, gratitude, admiration, desire, etc. cannot be replaced by theoretical or practical equivalents.

The remedy to the dangers and distortions of emotional responses must not be sought in conceptuality or in disinterested observation of empirical facts, but in more appropriate responses emerging from a more appropriate, more open and authentic, truthful and pure affectivity. Purification of the ways in which we let ourselves be affected, and—more primordially— purification of our *being* tuned to the various levels and instances of phenomenality, are necessary conditions for thinking in accordance with reality.

To be in tune, such that the appropriate responses are given, presupposes a turning away from inauthentic positions and movements in which we are immersed. Without conversion, no affective or other purification, and thus no authentic thought, is possible. Perception and thinking start from an urge for authenticity; they represent a specific form of ongoing conversion and catharsis.

If it is true that philosophy can neither be practiced nor understood as a passionless and emotionless exercise in rationality, it is led by a drive and a passion other than the typically modern preoccupation with scientificity and objective theory. The recognition of its emotional character is not a plea for subjectivism in philosophy, for with the absolutization of objectivity the alternative absolutization of subjectivity has also come to an end. Life and selfhood themselves, like all other phenomena, call for ongoing experimentation through which the quality of our experiences is at stake. To live philosophically is to exercise responsiveness to and responsibility for genuine ways of being touched and moved. If philosophy encompasses a basic responsibility for authentic affectivity, including a constantly adjusted orientation toward that for which a life ultimately is meant, philosophy is a specific form of spirituality. Its specificity lies in the "organ," the logic and the method through which it is distinguished from other, nonphilosophical forms of practice, speech, meditation, or contemplation. However, this specificity need not hide its belonging to a long tradition of moral and religious self-transformation. Important historical studies by Festugière, Courcelle, Hadot and others[5] have laid the ground for the possibility of continuing the premodern traditions of philosophy as a way of life, broken off by modern theory. Theory, in the restricted, modern sense of the word, must again be practiced and understood as only one of the elements of an entire life on the way to its own transformation. The theoretical perspective is merely a part, and often not the most important part, of human responsiveness and thoughtful experience. The language of logic, in the widest sense of this word, must unfold in the closest possible proximity to the language of desire and engagement. The passion of life, in its attempts at authentic purity, must be heard in the fine-tuned analyses and argumentations of a highly sensitive theory. The main issue is "correspondence": a well-tuned accord between the life of the self, and the various modes of being. It encompasses philosophical theory and tests how true it is to the nontheoretical moments of life's experience—some of which are more basic than theory.

Tasks

"The end of philosophy," proclaimed by several thinkers of our century, is in fact the end of *modern* philosophy and the beginning of a new, promising era in which the tasks and promises of philosophy have to be pursued on a new basis. We are not ungrateful for the lessons of the last 400 years, if we interpret modern philosophy as an experiment whose discoveries made us forget a wiser tradition of thought. As search for wisdom, philosophy was much more than theory. The Greek enlightenment certainly stressed contemplation *(theoria)* as a most divine possibility of human existence, but it never forgot the vital unity of *theoria* with practical nobility and emotional harmony. With the advent of Christianity, the spiritual orientation changed and the importance of thinking was relativized with respect to religious contemplation; love *(agapē)* and grace became more important than *epistēmē;* still, theory was venerated as a part of the dynamic that belongs to human maturity and perfection.

Many tasks are waiting for Christians who are passionate, skilled and courageous enough to rethink the basic issues of our existence in history. One of those tasks lies in a new assessment of the relations between wisdom, life and theory, and the realization of a phenomenology that does justice to those experiences that have been obscured or distorted by the modern and premodern theory. Two issues especially demand to be treated with greater respect and sensitivity than they have received in the past: human intersubjectivity and our relationship to God.

The work of Emmanuel Levinas has clarified some of the phenomenological difficulties concerning the appearance of human individuals.[6] As soon as I objectify, thematize, or simply talk *about* an other's face or speech or gesture, the other's otherness, as experienced in my greeting, listening and looking, disappears. The following problem then arises: how is it possible to philosophize about the other's existence and my relation to the other without distorting the very topic or theme I am trying to bring to light? How can my talking *about* the other remain a part of my listening or talking *to* the other? To "save the phenomenon" of the other, we must invent a language, or perhaps more than one language, that overcomes the deficiencies of pure theory. The fact that 2,500 years of Western philosophy have not yet done justice to the otherness of the other is already reason enough to believe that philosophy has not yet reached its end. It has hardly begun. Indeed, "intersubjectivity"—as we say much too easily—is not just one topic among others. The question of "you-ness" and "mineness" involves us in attempts to find a radically new interpretation of our relationship to one another and to society, as well as new interpretations of our relationship to God, to whom we refer, again much too easily, as a person.

Our relationship to God confronts us with an as yet unresolved problem of its own. Doesn't all talk *about* God miss the point, while talking *to* God, as in prayer, is a natural and appropriate response to his being? Isn't adoration, including gratitude, love and hope, the heart of all responsiveness with respect to God? St. Augustine, St. Anselm, St. Bonaventure and other Christian philosophers have thought about this question, but their answers are no more than hints.

It is obvious that a more faithful rendering of our relationships to God and other humans would have profound consequences for all other questions in philosophy. Philosophy is not exhausted at all; it is eager to start again. In the meantime, however, I do not want to suggest that the continuation of philosophy depends on the emergence of new problems and tasks. Even if only the same old questions persist, they must be meditated upon again and again. The most important questions of human life probably do not change, but every epoch has its own tasks and possibilities.

Autonomy

I can be brief with regard to the third feature of modern philosophy, its autonomy. All the great thinkers after Hegel have shown to what extent philosophy is rooted in prephilosophical desires, symbols, convictions and traditions. This does not necessarily require us to reject the ideal of autonomy proclaimed in modern philosophy: despite the failures of the past, it might still be possible to demonstrate the truth of presupposed convictions on the basis of empirical and logical evidence alone. However, all the holes and unproved assumptions which we have discovered in the Herculean works of the last centuries have made us very dubious about the feasibility of the autarchic program they wanted to realize. If we connect this doubt with the question of the difference between philosophy as a way of life and philosophy as theory, it becomes more plausible that the idea of rational autonomy is an illusion. It might still serve as a regulative idea, but as dogmatic affirmation of philosophy's autonomy it has exhausted itself.

If philosophical theory cannot be practiced without a deeply rooted passion, the word "faith" is not too strong to express the involvement of a real philosopher. Notwithstanding its own interpretation of philosophy as objective theory, the adventure of modern philosophy has in fact been motivated by a desire for wisdom and salvation.[7] Just as for "the Greeks," so also for most modern thinkers, and even for some scientists, philosophy replaces religion. At the source of all lives there is a sort of wager with ourselves, a lived, preconscious and certainly pretheoretical affirmation which takes the risk of being oriented in a certain direction and tries to accomplish a certain task as well as possible. Perhaps we might use the word "religion" in a very fundamental sense to stand for the attachment—a kind of Amen—that makes it possible for us to undertake the adventure that constitutes the course of our life. The adventurous history of rational theory and scientificity is supported and motivated by that pretheoretical and subconscious engagement.

The hidden faith that guides a life is expressed in its anticipations and disappointments, its joys and delights, and the stubborn responsibility with which its project is achieved. Moods and emotional dispositions, imaginative associations and conceptual preferences can be interpreted as symptoms of that faith. No artist, scientist or philosopher is without faith; hence it is an important question of philosophy to ask how their faith relates to their skills and to the way of life in which those skills play an important role.

II. Christianity

Before we ask whether a particular kind of philosophy or philosophy in general can or should be Christian, we must agree on the meaning of "Christian." While "Christian," "Christianity" and "Christendom" can be used to point at a cultural and historical phenomenon, "faith," in its biblical meaning, is a gift that does not belong to any particular culture. It is peculiar neither to a particular theological or philosophical, dogmatic or catechetic formulation, nor to a specific ethos. Christian faith certainly demands its concretization in appropriate ethical, communitarian and cultural traditions and institutions, but the inevitable particularity and historicity of all concretizations suggests a fundamental ambiguity in the word "Christian." Many different communities and practices are Christian, but it is their common faith alone which unites them as varieties in place and time. The Christianity of Western civilization is different from the evangelical picture of Jesus' "small herd." Already the oldest documents present various versions of evangelical life. To what extent these versions contain elements of human sinfulness, is a question I shall not address here, but it is obvious that, for instance, the Church of the crusades, the Church of the Inquisition and the Church of absolute monarchism can only be called Christian on the condition that we understand it as an indication of our "being just and sinners simultaneously." All this must be said in the name of faith itself, but as soon as we try to formulate this supreme criterion, our formulations and applications are indebted to a particular culture for the concretization of faith and the "purity of the holy Gospel."

"Christian" culture is always a mixture; the lives of Christians are attempts and experiments in appropriating the Spirit's inspiration, despite our unavoidable participation in a particularizing and contaminating world. Christian faith itself remains hidden in a host of historical, situational and biographical ways of concretization and partial distortion. To be a Christian is to live an adventure, continually searching for the pure source of grace. Without mixture, in its precultural purity, the Trinitarian faith in God and incarnation would not exist at all; its translation into language, behavior, ethos, myths, ideas, arts and idols is a persistent battle between contamination and purification. The purity of the gospel does not consist of an unworldly or supracultural or unhistorical spiritualism; the human body in its world and history is sanctified by grace. What we ambiguously call "spirituality" does not aim at a separation or destruction of the body, as if the body were a corpse, but at total transfiguration. To follow saints and prophets is a sustained search for the authenticity of the appropriate call.

The incarnatory structure of faith has two sides which are not easy to balance, as the history of Christian spirituality shows. On the one hand, grace maintains a distance from the world—God is our temple, and in heaven there is neither sacrament nor law— but, on the other hand, the whole of creation is called to union with God's life and has already begun to participate in it. This tension between distance and participation expresses itself in an individual Christian life as the tension between love for and detachment from the finite, admiration *and* "contempt for the world,"[8] passion *and* indifference, solidarity *and* patience, even with regard to the most urgent demands.

With regard to the Christian community of faith, a similar tension can be observed. As the "mystical body of Christ," the Christian community is sanctified and guided by the Spirit. The hope that surges from this certitude permits us to be at home in the world. Jesus the Christ is not "Yes" and "No," but only "Yes." It is in him only that we can say *"Amen"* (2 Cor 1:19–20). In the course of history *(in via)* it is not so easy to identify the community of Jesus Christ, however, and it is even more difficult to determine who truly belongs to it. But even if we are able to do this, it is obvious, and an element of faith itself, that the historical community of Christians also participates in the idols and sins of the world. Among those idols are the various forms of absolutization on all levels of culture, such as dogmatic fixations on a particular ethos, thought, taste or government.

Christians who desire to become more authentic cannot go the way of purification, unless they first belong to a Christian community from which they hear and learn how to respond to the call of God in Jesus through the Spirit. The education they receive from those who pass on what they received from others is a particular and contaminated translation of grace and faith, but without initiation and catechesis nobody would be able to arrive at the truth of revelation. A Christian life begins in a mixture of faith, culture and sin, in which faith is the critical element that rejects sin by forbidding any absolutization of culture. This rejection holds even if faith has become tightly attached to its translation into a particular ethos or doctrine. The faith that breaks all idols has been alive "from Abel on,"[9] and will remain alive in many forms inside and outside the communities of those who call themselves Christian.

Faith urges us to progressively overcome our idolatrous attachments to particular forms of human culture. Yet how can we distinguish between the purity of faith and its investment in the variety of "human-all-too-human" concretizations? The "sense of faith" by which to distinguish it from its cultural concretization cannot be learned in a few lessons. We are fortunate when the family or the church in which we were educated had good taste in questions and practices of faith, but even then it takes time for us to acquire an appreciation for what is and is not essential. It is the living experience and the achievement of Christian life itself which test the quality of this very experience. The Spirit creates receptive hearts through the self-critical experience of Christians. The "discernment of spirits"[10] is not guaranteed by repetition or imitation of words or deeds; a good sense or taste for things of the Spirit is a charism without which purification is impossible. A Christian trusts that God will not deceive anyone to whom he gave a good beginning. Grace procures all that is necessary for an appropriate response, but such a response cannot emerge without passionate concentration on that same grace through gratitude, hope, and adoration.

At this point we could meditate on the possibilities of the "inner master" of whom Saint Augustine and Saint Bonaventure speak.[11] If Christians are governed by faith, wouldn't they recognize the voice of the Spirit as being radically different from the voices of literature, art, morality, philosophy and theology? Spirituality is an ongoing experiment in which one experiences, tastes, and tests various stages and levels of experience; it is a movement toward greater authenticity. Self-testing is the natural way in which grace produces a more sensitive and refined mind or "heart." Through remembering and recognition, critique and transformation, the hermeneutical praxis of Christianity generates its more or less genuine styles of life.

The means used in this process of authentification are sometimes surprising. If faith in the God of Jesus Christ is not restricted to Christians, as the letter to the Hebrews declares, the very faith in the triune God has led the saints of all times, from Abel to the end of history.[12] The charismata of God's incarnation have been given to many non-Christians before and after Jesus' life. Examples of such gifts can be found in the modern declarations of human rights and the legal treaties that issued from them. The fact that the popes of the 20th century support and spread the doctrine of universal human rights is not primarily due to the practice or theory of former popes; it is rather the modern ethos of law and morality, as expressed by philosophers and lawyers both without and within the Christian community. The fact that the community of Christians recognizes an extra-Christian development as a welcome translation of its own faith shows that the borderline between Christianity ("faith") and non-Christian elements of faith is not easy to draw. Many who seem to be outside are inside (and many who seem to be inside are outside). While it is true that the meaning of a practice or an idea might change through being integrated into a Christian context, it may emerge outside that context. It makes a difference whether human rights are seen as founded on human autonomy alone, or whether they are recognized as a partial expression of God's concern, but this difference does not take a certain affinity away.

Another example already mentioned is the transformation of Platonic or Neoplatonic thought into elements of Christian theology from Origen to the late Middle Ages. Historical aspects of that transformation have been analyzed by the best scholars in the field. We have thus become aware of our debt to "the Greeks," but are we able to formulate a general theory about the integration of non-Christian philosophy into a Christian life?

III. Christian Philosophy

Christians who are also philosophers cannot avoid the question of how they can be both. How does philosophy fit into my existence as a member of the Christian community in search of God? How does my being a Christian fit into my philosophical search for truth? Different perspectives and positions can be chosen to answer these questions (or to amend them in order to answer better targeted questions). In a purely formal way, we can approach them in three ways: 1) we can try to integrate philosophy into the experience of Christian life; 2) we can try to integrate Christian faith into the philosophical way of life; and 3) we can try to show that the Christian way of life and philosophy remain two different and largely separate movements, despite a certain overlap. For a Christian who is involved in philosophy, an absolute separation is excluded from the outset if both philosophy and the Christian way are serious enterprises, for how could such a person otherwise maintain the basic unity of such a life?

1. Fides quaerens intellectum

If "philosophy" is taken in the restricted sense of a skill with a technique of its own, it would seem easy to solve our problem. "Christian philosophy" would designate a group of Christians who, like anybody else, have learned how to handle the tools of description, definition, analysis and synthesis developed in the history of logic, ontology, ethics, and so on. Their specificity is that they apply logical, linguistic, imaginative and rhetorical techniques to the convictions that are proper to their faith, just as Buddhists or Hindus might do. The only difference between Christian and other thinkers would lie in their particular synthesis of various tools with the religious truths that constitute their faith tradition. Their synthesis could then be called "theology," in the sense of a doctrine that explicitly appeals to extra-philosophical truth(s) as a basis for thinking.

The history of ontology and philosophical theology that

stretches from Parmenides to Levinas shows that this view of the relation between Christianity and philosophy is too superficial. Philosophy has never been a merely formal enterprise. Even if philosophy is restricted to theoretical endeavors, it cannot avoid thinking about the conditions of its own possibility, such as the ways in which logical and linguistic skills and strategies are related to the realities to which they are "applied," the modes of appearance and being of those realities, and the wonder of their givenness. Philosophy has always been, in some sense of the word, onto-theo-logy; all classical philosophers were fascinated by Being and by God. Under various names and pseudonyms, God and Being were the focus of their thinking.

The onto-theo-logy developed in philosophy cannot be seen as neutral and undecided with regard to a Christian addition or extension. "The God of the philosophers" is either a rival or a shadow of the God adored in faith and respected in theology, and differences in the understanding of God entail radical differences in ontology. Christian "faith in search of understanding" cannot simply adopt a non-Christian philosophy in order to add new truths to it; the Christianity of theology demands a more radical transformation. No philosophy is neutral; every philosophy, Christian or not, even an atheist philosophy, is oriented and ruled by a fundamental affirmation, a "Yes and Amen," that supports and colors all its essential affirmations. The integration of a non-Christian philosophy in a Christian theology demands therefore a profound rethinking of its assumptions and arguments. This rethinking must itself be inspired by another Amen: God as revealed in Jesus Christ. The enlightened faith sought by Christian theology regenerates the thoughts it adopts, while producing itself as a *"philosophia"* in the service of Christ.[13] Through the submission of intelligence to the obedience to faith,[14] all phenomena and thoughts change into manifestations of God's glory.

Faith in search of understanding is one of the ways in which the Christian community continues the assumption of the human world, made possible by the Incarnation. In a civilization where philosophy has become an important mode of coping with the drama of human existence, this pursuit is a normal kind of search. As the yeast of the world, faith appropriates the key elements of existing civilizations. The field of research that opens at this point invites us to analyze the structure of the conversion and the movement of transfiguration through which intellectual life becomes an element of faith. The patristic and medieval thematizations of the soul's journey, the mystical experiences of the sixteenth century, the Hegelian phenomenology of the Spirit's discoveries, Kierkegaard's stages on the way of life, etc. are highlights of a tradition that must be continued and renewed if we want to understand how philosophy, or thinking in general, can or must play a role in the maturation of faith.

2. Christian and Philosophical Ways of Life

If philosophy is the engagement in a specific way of life, more radical than any theory, the problem of Christian philosophy is whether the Christian way can be combined with an authentic involvement in philosophy. Since such an involvement can only be passionate, we must answer the question of whether love of God is compatible with a profound passion for philosophy.

a) *From the perspective of Christian faith,* philosophy is not a necessary kind of existence. Since all humans are called upon to participate in grace, the ability to philosophize cannot be a condition of its possibility. In a civilization where philosophy has become an essential moment of the prevailing culture, however, engagement in philosophy is one of the charismata through which the Christian community realizes its incarnatory character. At least some of its members must therefore participate in the history of the philosophical search for wisdom and human perfection. Which Christians become philosophers is a question of vocation, just as prophets, priests and artists are called to their kinds of charismatic life.

However, if it is true that authentic philosophy implies a fundamental affirmation or trust, from which it draws the courage for its search, how then can the Christian faith in the unique Amen of grace be combined with that philosophical affirmation? For a Christian, the passion for a life of thinking and discussion cannot be ultimate, but it can be lived as a possible and enjoyable concretization of the decisive call to love.[15] Yet doesn't this presuppose an "imprisonment" of philosophical autarchy to "the obedience of faith"?[16] Can involvement in philosophy be converted into a specific mode of the Christian way, or can it only be enacted as a not-quite-serious game?

It is important to note that the question I am asking here does not set two different doctrines or practices in opposition. Faith establishes the Christian community in the truth of revelation, which, in some way, embraces and supports all truths discoverable by human reason, while the philosophical search for truth is a meditative way of living out the answers it finds *and the questions* it asks such that they are felt, understood, and incorporated in growing wisdom; it is a gradual, not only theoretical but also emotional and practical transformation of the philosopher. A Christian who engages in philosophy lives his faith in the contingent and historical form of a contemplation that was invented by the Greeks, but transformed by the Christians with the help of Romans, Jews, Muslims and modern thinkers, including agnostics and atheists.

Because Christian appropriation includes conversion and transfiguration, it is possible to recognize the philosophies of non-Christian origin with which various groups of Christians have been involved. Thus we can discern Christian forms of Platonism, Stoicism, Aristotelianism, Hegelianism, and so forth. In all such varieties, however, the symbiosis of faith and philosophy is experienced in the mode of the "as if not" which, according to Paul's first letter to the Corinthians, characterizes the transitoriness of this world's *"schēma"* or *"figura."*[17] The distance between grace and culture does not exclude their intimate synthesis, but this synthesis is not a necessary one; all attempts at translating into philosophy are tentative and provisional. The passion of philosophy and its Amen cannot replace or conquer the Amen of grace. Compassion is better than insight, but it does not dishonor or despise it.

Philosophy itself has discovered that it is not radically autonomous; contemporary relativism must be understood as an expression of its need for another, more radical Amen than the purely philosophical one. The search for wisdom is a search for the true name of the Yes that is somehow present in the trust and the courage without which the very search would be impossible. Revelation and faith do offer the primordial affirmation, but they do not abolish the philosophical search, its questions, and its radical trust; these are relativized however, and made provisional, by the grace of a compassion that does not need philosophy but frees it for the contemplation of delightful possibilities and limitations.

The freedom of grace realizes itself in absolute love for God's compassion and an authentic but mortal and controlled passion for a philosophical kind of life. Using logical and linguistic tools and experimenting with various modes of understanding, a Christian philosopher is engaged in a history of meditation and discussion, while remaining well aware of their provisionality.

The provisional character of all philosophies within the Christian context is one aspect of faith's phenomenality. The wider question must be asked of how faith becomes phenomenal in the philosophies of authentic Christians who are passionately involved in it, and how these philosophies differ from other, non-Christian philosophies. A theological phenomenology of historical philosophies is necessary to prepare a thematic answer to that question. Paul's "as if not" can guide us, if we do not mistake it for an exhortation to divorce or contempt.

b) *From the point of view of philosophy* we must ask whether a Christian engaged in a philosophical discussion can be taken seriously enough to be accepted as an interlocutor.

Since the modern ideal of philosophical autarchy has been abandoned, it is not easy to define or defend the universality of

philosophy. Insofar as it maintains essential relations with particular religions and cultures, philosophy seems to be radically frag-
mented. However, if it did not at least try to speak a language and
to think thoughts that are comprehensible to every human
being, philosophy would die. Somehow its universality must be
saved. Mathematics, the sciences, logic, technology, and econom-
ics have become universal languages, but it would be disastrous if
they constituted the only possibility for humankind's communication and wisdom.

To be involved in the search for wisdom is certainly an impassioned affair, but can we count on Christians to participate in it?
Don't they feel superior by having the right answers? Don't they
act like pastors or missionaries rather than companions in the
search?

As I have said, the answers of faith cannot replace questions
and answers of philosophy. Even if I believe in God as the source
of my salvation, I do not thereby have a philosophical concept of
God, nor do I necessarily have an insight into the structure of salvation, its relation to culture, and my desire for salvation. All
these questions concern also my non-Christian colleagues in philosophy, even if they do not pay attention to them. They too start
from personal assumptions and aspirations, when they ponder
them. We share a collection of opinions, hopes and orientations
that belong to the historical period and the situation in which we
live. That we are philosophers testifies to a common trust in the
possibility of approaching truth. Our interpretation of the primordial Amen might differ, but it creates a fundamental affinity.
Might we not surmise that for each of us the Amen hides the universal guidance of a hidden God whom we confess without clear
knowledge of what and how he is, nor how he guides?

While a faith that identifies itself with a particular philosophical
or theological doctrine is dogmatic and idolatrous in neglecting
the distance between faith itself and the translation of faith into
thought, a philosophy that despises the possibilities of faith
believes in its own superiority; it has its own faith. Philosophical
discussions are not possible unless the participants share common

questions and contexts, but their profoundest convictions need not be the same. Philosophy does not come into being *ex nihilo;* it begins when someone, in the midst of a full life, tries to restructure through thinking that same life with all its convictions, practices and feelings. A philosophizing Christian experiences participation in the philosophical debate as an involvement which, though seriously concerned with God, humankind, the world, truth and wisdom, cannot decide the ultimate meaning of human destiny. A Christian is not alone in this: in everyone's life there is a distinction between belief (or religion) and reason. As a way of life, the philosophical experience is close to the Amen of religion and faith; if its trust is ultimately motivated by God, it coincides fundamentally with the Amen of Christian faith; if not, it is idolatrous or a provisional stage of the search for Meaning. In the first case, philosophy might help to disclose the convergence of positions that seem to differ radically.

The *gnosis*[18] of faith has a different character than philosophical knowledge. Committed Christians are on the way to a better understanding of the revealed truth about the human universe, but this does not necessarily mean that they grow in conceptual possession or mastery. What we heard about God who shows his love in Passion and Resurrection frames an endless program for growth in the wisdom of love. Such a *gnosis* does not entail a phenomenological description or a conceptual analysis of what it means to be a Christian, although philosophical descriptions and analyses play a role in spiritual growth. As an enlightened kind of advancement, such techniques can serve to respond to the Spirit that moves beyond all knowledge. Neither theory nor a virtuous way of life can replace the adoration from which an authentic *gnosis* springs. However, a well-ordered life, and even, to some extent, good theories, are welcome as possible *"schēmata"* or *"figurae"* of God's embodiment.[19]

—//—

c) *The philosophical perspective is a desirable moment of the perspective of faith itself.*

Not only do philosophizing Christians participate in the discussions of humanity, but their philosophical engagement is also a necessary moment of their own theological self-reflection and that of the Christian community to which they belong. A philosopher cannot avoid meditation on the question: Who, how, why am I? In Christians, such meditations are characterized by gratitude, hope, patience, and adoration. Although a neutral mode of philosophy might not permit an accurate phenomenology of the Christian mode of existence in faith, it is a valuable way of discovering the difference between faith itself and its translation into cultural or biographical expressions. By participating in the practices, languages, theories, and emotional patterns of non-Christian philosophers, without appealing to the specificity of Christian faith, we accomplish an *epoch ̄e* which might enable us to discover the limits of our understanding and the infinity that lies beyond it. The overwhelming message of a loving and suffering God reveals its incredible grandeur when we have measured the totality of dimensions and possibilities that can be explored philosophically. Seriously oriented lives in the style of Plato and Spinoza, compared with those of, for instance, Francis of Assisi and Charles de Foucauld, demonstrate the distance between philosophers and saints, although a sort of unrecognized sainthood might also hide in some philosophical lives. The distinction between Christian theology and non-Christian philosophy must be maintained in order that the latter's tendency to idolatry and the former's tendency to dogmatism do not dominate the discussion. Theology too is threatened by idolatry, and one of the weapons we can use to overcome this danger is precisely a certain way of practicing philosophy. In order to grow in wisdom, both philosophy and theology must spring from patient receptivity and avoid arrogance. Sincere philosophy helps theology to discover how much it has borrowed from the non-Christian wisdom found in secular science, ethos, politics, literature, rhetoric and philosophy. This discovery does not *per se* exclude these borrowings from the patrimony of faith; on the contrary, it allows us to question the extent to which such appropriations must be accepted as appropriate to the historical situation of the Christian community and how much they ought to be retained once that situation has changed. Thus participation in the extra-Christian practice of philosophy can participate in the fight against fossilization and superstition within the Church, and so in its ongoing purification.

Many thinkers who opposed Christianity have in fact offered helpful criticisms against the lies and the violence, the resentments and the hypocrisy that have been perpetuated by Christians. Often their target was a caricature of Christianity, but the words and the deeds of many Christians seemed to justify such caricatures. It is a healthy, though painful, exercise to look with un-Christian eyes at philosophical parodies of the Christian community in different periods of its history and to notice their partial accuracy. It should spur us to do penance for many infantile and morbid, superficial and unjust, arrogant and idolatrous distortions of grace. Although these distortions have not destroyed the fundamental Amen on which the Church is built, they do testify to its contamination by human-all-too-human corruptibility. In no way, however, should the recognition of this contamination override the joyful gratitude of Christian philosophers for the spirit of grace which freed them for something better than absolute knowledge.

Christians who exclude their being what they are from philosophical discussions are not genuine; they are at best pale images of the best non-Christian philosophers. Imitation of modern and postmodern attempts at philosophical autarchy has damaged the authenticity of Christian thought, no less than the Church's condemnations of important developments in art, science, politics, law, and philosophy. A post-postmodern renaissance of Christian spirituality in philosophy is necessary.

X. Theology Between Science and Spirituality

For centuries, Western Christianity has defined theology as a thoughtful search for conceptual clarification of the truth that faith confesses. *Fides quaerens intellectum* is not only a formula for Augustine's method; it also identifies an approach that determined what was expected of theologians until well into the modern era. In the medieval *universitas scientiarum,* theology understood this way was considered the queen unto whom the rest of the sciences, led by philosophy, had to declare their respect. Since the rise and triumph of modern science, theologians have had to share more and more the fate of Christian priests and prophets. The queen has long been dethroned; however, the war of succession continues.

In the modern university, personal convictions and confessions were out of place. Piety and faith were kept in the background, in the domain of individual preferences and special societies. Academic truth, on the other hand, was considered to be universal. As the cathedral of scholarship, the university became the most prominent center of culture. Its esteemed scholars were the enlightened prophets of a new age. Acceptance in this illustrious society required a commitment to honor authority-free and unprejudiced scientificity. The basis of modern science was its emancipated autonomy, the desire to free oneself from bondage to any authority and unproven beliefs so as to be able impartially to discover or (re)construct the "objective" truth about all of reality. Theology, since it is explicitly based on sacred words and an a priori faith, seemed atavistic in the company of the modern sciences. Although it was tolerated with a smirk, it could hardly be considered a fully worthwhile science.

Options

In this situation, there were three possible ways for theology to avoid the scorn of the scientific elite. *First,* it could withdraw from academic society into an intellectual ghetto, fervently committing itself to a restricted and undisturbed contemplation within the safe confines of an isolated community so that it would no longer feel threatened by scientific criticism. By avoiding scientific discussions, theology risks the shriveling of its scholarly quality, but it can accept this if it is convinced that piety is better than scholarship.

A *second* option would be to claim a special status for theology by appealing to a widespread acceptance of the privileged testimonies that form the basis of its teachings. This rescue attempt failed once modern society, after dividing into a variety of Christian confessions, officially became non-Christian or secular. As long as the Christian character of European society was still uncontested, however, theologians could avail themselves of a distinction between those parts of theology that convey the common inheritance of all Christians in a commonly accepted manner, and other divisions that are essential to the life of certain denominations but irrelevant or erroneous for others.

The *third* option would be to adapt theology as much as possible to the postulates and demands of the modern sciences, including unprejudiced objectivity, freedom from authority, and neutrality.

Because Christianity lost the privilege of being considered the sole true religion, it became one of many in the universal museum of religions. Moreover, the phenomenon of religion as such was reduced to a pure fact, and the question whether a human life could be meaningful without religion was increasingly denied or unanswered. Since atheism has been accepted as a viable possibility, it is no longer possible to start from the idea that religion is obviously a normal and normative given.

Nothing prevents individual theologians as private persons from believing particular versions of Christianity, but as participants in the academic milieu they are supposed to play the game of impartiality and distance, as if the truth of God's existence and their own faith did not concern them profoundly. They may express their concern with truth by involving themselves in the *philosophical* debate over the meaning of religion and its coherence with the rest of human existence, but philosophy of religion, too, faces the challenge that its subject is considered alien or even irrelevant to the contemporary world.

As the scientific study of religious phenomena, theology has come to resemble a conglomerate of various disciplines, held together only by its common object and the modern style of its various methods. From philosophy of religion, through philology and the science of interpretation, to history, sociology, anthropology, and sociology of religion, theologians and their students proceed through a series of texts and interpretations, descriptions, analyses, and views that offer a glimpse into specific specimens of religion from a perspective that is emotionally unengaged but scientifically interested. There are two ways for scholars to immerse themselves in the significance and coherence of actual religious convictions: either as participants in faith who practice dogmatic theology in a time-honored (e.g., Augustinian) manner with the additional enrichment of modern skills, or as practitioners of science who bracket that specific faith in order to explain objectively what its adherents believe and practice. Does it make any difference whether believers seeking to clarify their faith commit themselves to one approach or the other?

Theology regained a degree of respectability through its transformation into a modern science. This respect relied not on the intensity of its faith, the elevation of its views, its concern for human misery, or the wisdom of its hints for the practice of daily life, but on the quality of its scholarship. Professionally capable theologians can compete with the best academicians of other faculties specifically in terms of the exegetical, historical, philosophical, or human-scientific products of their labor. Modern science can find nothing wrong with the methodological clarity of this kind of theology. The quality of its archaeological, philological, historical, psychological, sociological, and linguistic subdisciplines is impressive. Gratitude is due for the rich information they provide concerning the phenomena of religion and their role in human existence. Theological activity still causes suspicion in many nonbelieving intellectuals because of its subject, which seems illusory to them. Nevertheless, theologians can defend themselves against such suspicion just as well as do the theorists of literature, whose subject matter also contains myths and other fictions.

By becoming a science, modern theology seems to have become a collection of disciplines grouped together only because of their common subject matter. Does theology still have a point of view and a method of its *own*? If not, has it completely lost its former identity? Why does it continue to exist as a separate discipline? No single theologian can completely master all those other sciences in order to form an encyclopedic knowledge of religion. Wouldn't it be better to let the illusory coherence of its divisions disintegrate by delegating them to the various concerned departments? If, on the other hand, theology does have an identity and method of its own, in what does it consist? It cannot seek its identity in faith, since modern science requires this to be bracketed. Does theology have access to a special sort of experience and thinking?

The Scientific Ideal

Many admirers of the modern scientific type of rationality uncritically consider it to be the only form of rigorous scholarship. However, to avoid the danger of naïveté and superficiality, science should account for the unproven presuppositions implicit in its design. This would reveal, in contrast with its pretended autonomy and impartiality, a profound lack of neutrality, universal applicability, and sense of radical truth.

The self-understanding of modern science implies that it stands over and above the phenomena that are subject to its objectifying and dispassionate gaze. Its objects include many natural and cultural phenomena, including opinions, convictions, beliefs, and theories. The phenomena pass by the panoramic observation post of science, and scientists select what is to be studied with the various methods of their specialties, thus arranging the cosmos of things, relations, networks, intentions, and theories according to the presuppositions of their methods. Even the sciences themselves and those who practice them cannot be excluded from the cool gaze of scientific reflection. This must therefore develop a method for the understanding of the practices and the knowledge of the scientists. But can that method be the same as the one used for the movements of stones and muscles?

A first postulate of modern science is the thesis that it is possible for those who practice it to adopt a completely unprejudiced and autonomous standpoint. Only work produced in independence from any particular belief may properly be called scientific. Observation and theory must not be colored by subjective perspectives; if these cannot be avoided, a method must be devised to separate the true, objective, and universally valid core from these particular perspectives.

The modern scientific ideal resembles a modern museum. Thanks to the opening of the world and the survey of universal history we can in principle know everything. Yet this kind of omniscience makes it very difficult for us to believe in anything specific. With some exaggeration, we could say that we know everything, but believe nothing. Walking through the museum of all possible cultures, we look at innumerable phenomena, without attaching ourselves to any one of them. Each work of art or religion has a rightful place in the museum of humanity; each text has a place of equal value in our libraries. However, where would we find the right and the courage to declare some texts "very special," "the only true or good ones," or "better than all others"? How can we avoid becoming indifferent if we can no longer distinguish values or qualities? The products of humanity's imagination seem to have lost all other values than that of being objects of disinterested curiosity. Is the theoretical benefit of the modern sciences limited to encyclopedic information about homogeneous objects? Is this the result of the Western history of contemplation? Does theology end here, when it surrenders to the demands of modern science?

The contemporary call to societal relevance seems to be an attempt to oppose the sterility of scholarship that "does not reach the people." But "relevance" for what? Relevance for justice, well-being, and equal opportunities for fulfillment? As long as we do not know what a successful fulfillment of being human entails, as long as we do not know our most genuine needs and deepest desires, we do not possess a criterion for relevance. How then can we know what we should be seeking, whether in everyday life or scientific investigation?

The current call for spirituality is less vociferous than the social criticism of the '60s and '70s, but the desire for reflection and inspiration, emotion and passion is remarkable. However, many who have devoted themselves to the study of theology on account of such a desire are disappointed. In their opinion they have been sent away with the hard stones of scholarship instead of the bread they came seeking.

Many scholars find it tempting to refer such disappointments and the desires from which they arise to the private dimension of personal lives and subjective feelings or to the liturgical and pastoral concerns of ecclesiastical life. Separating the scientific side of theology from religious experience in all its affective and practical diversity miserably impoverishes theological thought while it risks to turn the experience into sentimentality. Only those who are genuine enough to entrust themselves to the naïveté of unreflected images and feelings have no problems with such a separation. However, more sophisticated believers find no rest until they have resolved the tensions between their faith and modern reason.

Separating lived life from the scientific study of religion is also untenable from the point of view of scholarship. No scholarly study of humanity can avoid questioning the relationships among experience, feeling, acting, thinking, loving, and willing as they are united in a single human existence. Scholars who isolate their specialty from human features that are studied by others are superficial or partial. It is not difficult to show how inconsistent the intellectual life of such a person is. All modern scholars, however, are faced with this situation to some extent, since our culture's ethos of specialization has caused an almost incurable separation of academic work and life.

If the scientistic consignment of everything existential to private rumination is a form of naïveté, another form is found in the aversion to theological scholarship that reacts by taking refuge in direct action and emotion. To oppose feeling and experience to the intellectual treatment of religious reality is to fall into the same dualism that is operative in quasi-scientific disregard for affectivity and wisdom. Polemics against the skilled rationality of modern theology in the name of emotions and inspiration, while absolutizing piety over against logically ordered reflection, do justice neither to the human character of religious experience nor to human *logos*. It is our task to analyze thoughtfully the interwovenness of our intellectual with our affective and practical responses. Reflecting on this will give us better insight into the possibilities and requirements of human rationality, thus enabling us to connect modern conceptuality with premodern insights into the affective dimension of thought. It will become evident that thinking is more radical and original than what modernity has made of it.

The often-quoted aphorism of Pascal, "The heart has reasons of its own that are unknown to reason,"[1] is merely a first hint with regard to the issue before us. In spite of its dualistic formulation, it correctly suggests that the core of human affectivity possesses its own kind of rationality. Reflection must uncover these reasons and show how rational thinking rises out of, while still remaining rooted in, an affective and practical ground that determines the orientation and the style of that thinking. Instead of an escape from reason into an ocean of feelings, symbols, and stories, true scholarship seeks to remain connected to the world of life experience and imagination, stories and poetry, moral praxis and religious celebrations, while also subjecting them to careful scrutiny, without denying their capacities of expressing a challenging mystery. Such an integrated way of thinking is no less rigorous than that of the modern sciences, including philosophy and theology. In fact, it is more reflective, since it expressly thematizes the rootedness of reason in the soil of lived lives rather than denying or neglecting it; at the same time, it does not take second place to the formal refinement of scientific logic, because it integrates this as an element of its own logic of an existential search for truth.

How can theology maintain its alliance with a faith-inspired life, without giving up its scholarly status? I see two possible strategies for answering this question.

From Scientific Neutrality to Involvement

The *first* strategy proceeds from a critique of the neutrality required by the modern ideal of science. It can be shown that such neutrality is impossible and that the allegedly attainable neutrality in fact masks a specific agenda, for example, an anticlerical or antireligious tradition issuing from the Enlightenment. The next step is to argue that every theology is necessarily founded in another engagement, and that its scholarly productivity can consist in nothing else than the rational elaboration of this engagement through critical discussions with itself and representatives of its own and other traditions. If we follow this approach, the following ideas demand attention.

As a first step, we must assert that no single interpretation of the human universe has been entirely impartial, universal and objective. Spinoza, Leibniz, Kant, and Hegel, for instance, were just as preoccupied by particular views and purposes in their philosophies as were Augustine and Pascal; their predispositions become clear as we closely analyze their work. Insofar as the various sciences are actual or potential parts of a comprehensive scientific whole, the thesis upheld here applies to every area of study that claims to express the truth about reality.

In the second step we defend that not only has neutrality been unattained, but that it is in principle impossible. To prove this thesis we need to develop a philosophical anthropology in which all human action is shown to spring from a radical desire that motivates all human formations and transformations. As with any other essentially human expression of life, our theoretical activity is inspired and dominated by a life project, at once unique and universally human. One's seeking and discovering (or failing to discover) truth gets its specific character from a peculiar way of existence. If it is true that our methodologies are shaped by various positions and by the dynamics of our most fundamental drives, modern scholarship's pretense of remaining objective and neutral cannot be true. Hence we must always be alert in asking which particular life project is displayed in any scholarly plan, and especially in those plans that are presented as impartial.

Earlier I compared modern science to a museum in which all the objects are displayed side-by-side, while it is left to the subjective appraisal of the visitors to decide which objects are the most interesting. This description is not exactly right, however. First of all, every museum has a hierarchy of places. The *Night Watch,* for example, hangs in a place of honor in the Dutch *Rijksmuseum* which thereby suggests that it is more prominent than other paintings by Rembrandt (a suggestion that might be debated).

Second, every museum is built in a particular style that is clearly recognizable as the style of a specific period and architect and thereby puts its objects into a context that might suit some of them better than others. Even a style that is very reserved so as not to interfere with the interpretation of the exhibits expresses a specific point of view inevitably anticipating certain elements of the interpretation.

What approach or perspective is expressed in the prevailing study of religion? Does it try, like our museums, to compensate for its own disengagement and indifference by displaying all kinds of equally "interesting" phenomena to our curiosity? What intention underlies scientific treatments of religious texts, institutions, codes, histories, and so on? Our culture seems to mourn over the fact that medieval culture did not surround every little piece of antiquity with a respectful railing or put it in a well-protected museum basement, but turned Roman forums into stone quarries for their Christian churches and replaced pagan idols by crosses and madonnas. Are we more civilized because we preserve all the (whole or half-ruined) products of cultures that are not our own? Do the modern ideals of objectivity and impartiality express awe for the works of the spirit or rather the skeptical sterility characteristic of a dying culture? Or is our banishment of all subjectivity the harbinger of a worldwide openness to the entire variety of peoples, cultures and faiths? As suspension of all judgments and decisions about truth and meaning, neutrality is an ambiguous ideal. It cannot become an independent standpoint, because human life cannot be satisfied with a multitude of "interesting" possibilities; these cannot provide a life with meaning unless they are transformed into concrete positions. The distance of a neutral and uncommitted gaze can only be a provisional stage or a subordinate moment in our progress to full engagement.

A complete justification for the line of thinking sketched here would require a theory of human existence as creative retrieval or hermeneutic praxis. Such a theory would demonstrate that human beings cannot restrict themselves to hypothetical visions;

they necessarily involve themselves in positions from which they evaluate and decide about the key issues of their existence. Such positions may cause many mistakes, but we cannot avoid making mistakes by refusing to identify with anything. Whatever reasons may motivate the attempt to maintain an uninvolved but sterile neutrality, the separation of scholarship from life uproots the former and obscures the latter.

A *second* strategy for revitalizing theology begins by inquiring how the formal structure of a scholarly methodology comports with the whole of human life. By dedicating ourselves to scholarship, we adopt a specific manner of realizing an essential element of human existence. If morality and religion are basic, then they will somehow be expressed in all our thinking, and thus also in its scholarly stylization. And since thinking is intertwined with the feeling, desiring, willing, and acting of a thinking person, the practice and the products of scholarship will also express what is going on in that person. Thinking and scholarship should therefore be evaluated, not only with regard to their technical or professional concerns but also from the perspective of their relations to the moral and religious quality of the life from which they emerge. Thinking, too, is an activity with many possible meanings: it may be part of a virtuous life-project, but it can just as well be an expression of vice. Aristotle's analysis of virtue as an attitude that disposes a person to the excellence of specific sorts of actions can be applied to scholarship as well. The "virtue" of good thinking is not constituted through the logical exactness of its formal skills and results alone; it demands also the well-attuned passion of *éros*. The discovery of truth is impossible without a proper orientation and inspiration.

This raises the question of the criterion for judging the moral and religious validity of theology. What spirit must inspire theology to make it not only scientifically justified, but also *good* (that is, borne from a good spirituality)? Since the deepest motives of human existence and thinking are at stake here, the inspiration we are seeking cannot be of neutral interest. A Christian answer to this question will emphasize that all intellectual work is ultimately connected with a radical relation of loving God "with all your heart, with all your soul, with all your mind, and with all your strength." The intellect of a true Christian cannot resist this kind of love, whereas the attitude of a completely autonomous science of religion is that of the self-conceit described in the first letter to the Corinthians.[2] As a version of self-justification it replaces the orientation to God by a passion for the autonomous self or other gods. In modern times, the most prominent candidate for such deification has been the "I" as prospective master and possessor of the earth.

Theological reflection gives expression to the kind of inspiration from which it emerges. In Christianity, the source of this inspiration is called "faith." Thus when Christian theology does not tear loose from its roots, it is faith in search of self-clarification: *fides quaerens intellectum.* Let us note once again that this conception of theology takes away none of the logical and methodical techniques developed by modern scholarship. These do not, however, constitute the supreme criterion for the significance of a theology, because they belong to a less radical dimension than that of inspiration and spirituality. Further refinement of descriptive, conceptual and interpretive methods remains necessary to translate the experience of faith onto the level of rigorous interpretation. In particular, the attempt to appeal as little as possible to unproven prejudices (the attempt to be as "objective" as possible) is a welcome component of self-examination from which no one is spared by "faith in search of insight." The cool gaze of rigorous science thus becomes a moment, though only a moment, of the experiment of a life lived in faith.

Christian theology is the thematically formulated *logos* of Christian experience. This formula must not be understood as an attempt to separate *logos* and experience from each other, however. The Christian experience is an ongoing process; it encompasses the entirety of a life in which logical elements are intertwined with practical and affective elements. In each stage of that process the characteristic experiences provoke new thoughts, as do transformations and impasses into which the various stages lead. Philosophy and modern science can be integrated into this adventure, earlier versions of which are described by Origen and Augustine, Ruusbroec and John of the Cross, Kierkegaard and many others.

Just as the path of Christian experience is not without *logos,* neither is the practice of *logos* in the context of a Christian life free from experience. Because the personal elements of a concrete life penetrate theological scholarship, the reading of theological texts must always be accompanied by attention to the spiritual tone that can be heard in them.

But have we yet mentioned God and faith at all? Experience, thinking, and the practice of scholarship are pursuits that belong to the domain of culture (and thus share the fate of all transitory historical realities) rather than to that of the most radical relation called faith. To what extent have we spoken about theology as a science of and for faith?

Faith itself eludes dissection by discursive analyses, but as the basis of a religious life it is expressed in characteristic forms of action, disposition, and perception. Gratitude and hope, for example, are empirical concretizations of faith in God as creator and redeemer. The empirical element in which faith appears, without giving up its mystery, is a mixture of images, words, affects, rituals, myths and histories that refer to an incomprehensible mystery. The factual form in which the mystery of faith is concretized is often a distortion, because many imperfect individuals, cultures, and times have left their traces in it. The study of these traces degenerates into idolatry when it forgets their link with the hidden "Sought."[3] Only faith itself judges the truth and the value of all the forms that present themselves as explanations or practices of faith. It cannot be identified with any interpretation, with any dogmatics, or with any word. Only the Spirit can bring words, dogmas, and interpretations to life.

To be sure, even theology has its idols. Its search for truth is a part of the lifelong experiment in which thinking, in union with desiring, and willing submit to an ever more radical purification. The discernment of forms of faith as mere forms encounters along its way the typical modern pattern of a panoramic view from an "interested" but uninvolved perspective. As an expression of our time, this pattern cannot resist nihilism. However, nihilism *can* be experienced as a dark night that prepares healing. If faith is not to let itself be trapped in dogmatics, the formless or "modeless" aspect of God must be respected. But such a manifestation is blinding, because God's modelessness is too much for us.[4] The light of such truth thus appears as a darkness in which almost nothing can be distinguished.

Not only an individual, but a period, too, can suffer from the formless hiddenness of God. The temptation to abandon the whole search for the Sought is then the greatest threat. Whoever does not want to give in but instead feels called to a courageous exodus follows a dark cloud. By night it contains a blinding fire, but by day, when other lights shine fully, smoke hides the burning core of its darkness. Holding fast to faith we find consolation in the canonical images and words that promise contact with the One who through them gives and withholds itself. Only a scholarly theology that is rooted in spirituality can realize the desired unity of faith and thought.

NOTES

I. Philosophy

1. Cf. G. W. F. Hegel, *Elements of the Philosophy of Right*, trans. H. B. Nisbet (Cambridge: Cambridge University Press, 1991), p. 23: "When philosophy paints it grey in grey, a shape of life has grown old, and it cannot be rejuvenated, but only known, by the grey in grey of philosophy." (I have corrected "recognized" for *erkennen* into "known." All translations in this book are my own, unless otherwise noted.) Hegel refers here to J. W. Goethe's *Faust* I, where Mephistopheles says to the student:

> Grey, dear friend, is all theory,
> and green the golden tree of life.

II. The Quest for Meaning

1. *Alcibiades* 120d, 123d, 127e–135e; *Apology* 36c; *Laches* 179d; *Phaedo* 62d, 115b; *Theaetetus* 153b.

144

2. *Alcibiades* 128d ff.; *Apology* 29e, 32d; *Phaedo* 107c; Martin Heidegger, *Being and Time,* tr. John Macquarrie and Edward Robinson (New York: Harper, 1962), §41.

3. If one is suspicious of the explicit or implicit self-conception of a particular school of thought, one can neither presume that the definitions of meaning or philosophy given in that school are correct, nor dogmatically replace all given definitions with definitions of one's own. At the beginning of this book, I cannot therefore rely on any "orthodox" definition of "philosophy" or "meaning," but I can appeal to the reader's and my own use of ordinary language, in which both words have many meanings, without immediately replacing the meaning of "meaning" and "philosophy" by "analytic," "idealist," "postmodern," "medieval" or other assumptions and interpretations. This does not mean that my understanding of these (and many other) words is neutral and impartial or that I would be able to stand above the parties, but it does allow for a discussion with other— equally partial—conceptions and assumptions.

4. The expression *"Sinngebung,"* central in Edmund Husserl's phenomenology of meaning, suggests too strongly that consciousness ultimately is actively constitutive. Without primordial receptivity, human consciousness could not even begin to act.

5. Aristotle, *Nicomachean Ethics* I, 10 (1100a 10 ff.).

6. Aesopus, "The Braggart" in *Aesopica,* ed. B. E. Perry (Urbana: University of Illinois Press, 1952), p. 334, and Hegel's use of it in his *Elements of the Philosophy of Right,* pp. 21–22, as explained in my *Philosophy and Politics: A Commentary on the Preface to Hegel's Philosophy of Right* (The Hague-Boston: Nijhoff, 1987), pp. 104–07 and 135–36.

V. The Relevance of Natural Theology

1. The solidarity between the God of natural theology and a judicial moralism is obvious in the Dialectic of Kant's *Critique of Practical Reason* (1788) and his *Religion within the Limits of Pure Reason* (1793).

2. This can be shown through a careful and meditative reading of classical texts about the ultimate referent, such as Plato, *Republic* 378e–383c and 508a–509b; Aristotle, *Metaphysics* XII, 9 (1074b15–1075a12); Plotinus, *Ennead* VI, 9; Descartes, third meditation of the *Metaphysical Meditations;* and Spinoza, Book V of the *Ethics.*

3. Cf., e.g., Anselm, *Proslogion,* chap. 15: "Therefore, Lord, you are not only that than which no greater can be thought; rather you are something greater than what can be thought." An explanation of the *Proslogion* in light of this conclusion and in contrast with Hegel's onto-theo-logy can be found in my "Anselm's Proslogion and its Hegelian Interpretation," *The St. John's Review* 42 (1993): 59–77. Cf. also this declaration in the *Constitutio de errore abbatis Joachim* of the fourth Lateran Council (1215): "Between the creator and the creatures no similitude can be found that cannot be surpassed by a greater dissimilitude." *Enchiridion symbolorum definitionum et declarationum de rebus fidei et morum,* 37th ed., ed. Heinrich Denzinger and Peter Hünermann (Freiburg: Herder, 1991), n. 806, p. 361.

4. When revising this text, Brian Chrzastek kindly completed this thought with the following sentences: "Faith, no matter how ardent, must remain open to the *possibility* that it is wrong. Thus a dynamic faith, one that continues to seek a deeper understanding of itself, is always at risk. It may lose itself in the doubts raised by self-examination (*non credo quia absurdum est*) or it may become more profound (*credo ut intelligam*)."

5. See Thomas Aquinas, *Summa Theologica* I, qu. 2, art. 3, *corpus:* "et hoc omnes intelligunt Deum," "quam omnes Deum nominant," "quod omnes dicunt Deum," "et hoc dicimus Deum."

6. Cf. Henri de Lubac in *Sur les chemins de Dieu* (Paris: Aubier-Montaigne, 1956), p. 191: "One cannot find God except by always seeking Him. God always remains 'the Sought'." De Lubac alludes here to Gregory of Nyssa's *Life of Moses* II, 162–165, where Gregory describes Moses' obscure knowledge of God as *to zētoumenon* (163).

VI. Religion and Experience

1. See, e.g., Saint Augustine, *Soliloquies* I, 7: Reason: What do you want to know? Soul: All that I have asked for in my prayer. Reason: Summarize it briefly. Soul: I want to know God and the soul. Reason: Nothing more? Soul: Nothing at all.

2. Henri de Lubac's *Catholisme. Les aspects sociaux du dogme* (Paris: Cerf, 1937) remains a monument of this rediscovery.

3. See chap. 1, n. 1.

4. For this interpretation of Plato's "idea," see Adriaan T. Peperzak, *Platonic Transformations: with and after Hegel, Heidegger, and Levinas* (Lanham, Md.: Rowman & Littlefield, 1997), pp. 13–14, 104–06, 143–45.

5. Cf. the *Histoire d'une âme,* published in 1898 under the name of Soeur Thérèse de l'Enfant-Jésus and reproduced in *La première 'Histoire d'une âme' de 1898* in *Edition critique des oeuvres complètes de Sainte Thérèse de l'Enfant-Jésus et de la Sainte-Face* (Paris: Cerf, 1992).

6. Cf. Heidegger's *Aus der Erfahrung des Denkens* (1947) and the collection in which it, with other short texts written between 1910 and 1976, has been published in Martin Heidegger, *Gesamtausgabe* I, vol. 13 (Frankfurt/Main: Klostermann, 1983).

7. I allude here to the *Gestalten des Geistes* of Hegel's *Phenomenology of the Spirit* (*Gesammelte Werke* [Hamburg: F. Meiner, 1968–], vol. 9).

8. This was the first title of Hegel's *Phenomenology of the Spirit*; see *Gesammelte Werke* g, pp. 444 and 469–71.

9. See Hegel's inaugural lectures at the University of Heidelberg (1816) and the University of Berlin (1818) in *Gesammelte Werke,* vol. 18, pp. 6, 18.

10. I use this word to characterize Hegel's system as a philosophy of absolute identity that is at the same time a *philosophy of the whole* (the truth is only in the whole) and—because of its claim that the entire truth can be deduced from its beginning—a *tautology.* A justification of this characteristic can be found in Adriaan Peperzak, *Selbsterkenntnis des Absoluten: Grundlinien der Hegelschen*

Philosophie des Geistes, vol. II.6 of *Spekulation und Erfahrung* (Stuttgart-Bad Cannstatt: Frommann-Holzboog, 1987), pp. 111–65 and "Selbstbewußtsein-Vernunft-Freiheit-Geist," in Lothar Eley, ed., *Hegels Theorie des subjektiven Geistes in der "Enzyklopädie der philosophischen Wissenschaften im Grundrisse,"* vol. II. 14 of *Spekulation und Erfahrung* (Stuttgart-Bad Cannstatt: Frommann-Holzboog, 1990), pp. 281–90.

VII. What Is Philosophy of Religion?

1. See Thomas Aquinas, *Summa Theologica* I, qu. 12, art. 12.

2. In Hegel's sense of the *Verstand* as opposed to the "speculative" logic of the *Vernunft.*

3. I use "empirical" as an equivalent of "experiential." Nobody is obliged to restrict the meaning of "empirical" to an exclusive property of modern science. Philosophers rather appeal to Aristotle's concept of *empeiria,* whose range is much wider, though not yet wide enough. The most authentic texts of the most authentic mystics, for example, show how far the dimension of the empirical extends.

4. Pascal, *Pensées,* n. 277, in Léon Brunschvicg's edition of Pascal, *Pensées et opuscules* (Paris: Hachette, s.d.) and n. 477 in *L'oeuvre de Pascal (Bibl. de la Pléiade),* ed. Jacques Chevalier (Paris: Gallimard, 1936), p. 963.

VIII. Philosophy and Faith

1. See, e.g., *Alcibiades* 130c and chap. 2, nn. 1, 2.

2. See *Apology* 30d–e and the entire *Phaedo.*

3. Dionysius, *Mystica Theologia* I, 1.

4. See chap. 5, n. 3.

5. Bonaventure, *Itinerarium mentis in Deum* VII, 5. For the first quote I made use of, but revised, the translation of Philotheus Boehner in vol. 2 of the *Works of Saint Bonaventure,* ed. Philotheus Boehner and Frances Laughlin (Saint Bonaventure, N.Y.: The Franciscan University, 1956), p. 98.

6. René Descartes, *Œuvres de Descartes,* ed. Charles Adam and Paul Tannery, rev. ed., 12 vols. (Paris: Vrin, 1964–76), vol. IX, *Méditations Métaphysiques,* pp. 41–42.

7. Descartes, *Œuvres,* vol. VI, *Discours de la Méthode,* pp. 6, 8, 28; vol. IX, *Méditations Métaphysiques,* pp. 4–8.

8. Descartes, "Letter of the author to him who translated the book, which letter can here serve as preface" (1647). The entire letter, as also Descartes' letter to Princess Elisabeth, which prefaced the Latin edition of the *Principia* of 1644, insists on the meaning of philosophy as the study of *wisdom.*

9. See Descartes, *Œuvres,* vol. VI, *Discours de la Méthode,* p. 62: "...to make ourselves the masters and possessors of nature."

10. In my interpretation of the postmedieval history of philosophy, modernity finishes with Hegel's failed attempt at constructing a complete synthesis of all preceding philosophy. Postmodernity begins then with Feuerbach, Marx, the later Schelling, and Kierkegaard.

11. Plotinus, *Ennead* V, 1, 1 in *Works,* vol. 5, tr. A. H. Armstrong (Cambridge, Mass.: Harvard University Press, 1984).

12. Rom 1:21–22.

13. 1 Cor 2:10–11.

IX. The Problem of Christian Philosophy

1. See chap. 6, n. 9. At *Gesammelte Werke,* vol. 18, p. 6 we read: "Faith in the power of the spirit is the first condition of philosophy."

2. I have tried to show this for Anselm in "Anselm's Proslogion and its Hegelian Interpretation," *The St. John's Review* 42 (1993): 59–77; for Descartes in "Life, Science and Wisdom according to Descartes," *History of Philosophy Quarterly* 12 (1995): 133–53; for Leibniz in "Dieu et la souffrance à partir de Leibniz," *Theodicea Oggi? Archivio di Filosofia* 56 (1988): 51–74; for Hegel in *Le jeune Hegel et la vision morale du monde* (The Hague: M. Nijhoff, 1969) and in "Existenz und Denken im Werden der Hegelschen Philosophie," *Scholastik* 38 (1963): 226–38; and for

Levinas in "Judaism according to Levinas," in my *Beyond: The Philosophy of Emmanuel Levinas* (Evanston, Ill.: Northwestern University Press, 1997), pp. 18–37.

3. I presuppose here the phenomenological critique of the subject-object schema: though it has its legitimate use within certain limits for certain domains of knowledge, it is incapable of constituting a universal framework.

4. Cf. Spinoza, *Tractatus de intellectus emendatione* and its explanation in Herman de Dijn's *Spinoza: The Way to Wisdom* (West Lafayette, Ind.: Purdue University Press, 1996).

5. Arthur Darby Nock, *Early Gentile Christianity and its Hellenistic Background* (New York: Harper & Row, 1964); *Conversion: The Old and the New in Religion from Alexander the Great to Augustine of Hippo* (Oxford: Clarendon Press, 1933); *Essays on Religion and the Ancient World* (Cambridge: Harvard University Press, 1972); Pierre Paul Courcelle, *Les lettres grecques en Occident, de Macrobe à Cassiodore* (Paris: E. de Boccard, 1948); *Connais-toi toi-même, de Socrate à Saint Bernard* (Paris: Études Augustiniennes, 1974); Pierre Hadot, *Exercises spirituels et philosophie antique* (Paris: Études Augustiniennes, 1987); *Qu'est-ce que la philosophie antique?* (Paris: Gallimard, 1995).

6. I have presented his work in *To the Other: Introduction to the Philosophy of Emmanuel Levinas* (West Lafayette, Ind.: Purdue University Press, 1993) and *Beyond: The Philosophy of Emmanuel Levinas*. For a discussion of his phenomenology of intersubjectivity, see *To the Other*, pp. 167–84; *Beyond*, pp. 123–29; and *Before Ethics* (Atlantic Highlands, N.J.: Humanities Press, 1997), pp. 47–53, 69–72.

7. For Descartes, see chap. 8, n. 8 and n. 2 of the current chapter. With regard to Spinoza (see n. 4), the title of his *Ethica* and the prefaces of its last three books already testify to this desire and purpose. It would be easy to show the same for Leibniz, Kant, Fichte, and Hegel, but most moderns see wisdom as very close to knowledge.

8. *Contemptus mundi* is a perversion if it is not motivated by admiration and gratitude toward the Creator whose gifts are

good and enjoyable. The negative moment of detachment, sacrifice and looking down must express the infinite distance between the finite and its infinite source, not declare or treat it as bad or despicable. However, it demands much practice to reach a pure sense of the difference between God and God's imitations (from the most sublime gods to the lowest demons).

9. This topos of the patristic literature comments on Heb 11:4ff.

10. See "Discernement des esprits" in *Dictionnaire de spiritualité ascétique et mystique, doctrine et histoire* (Paris: G. Beauchesne et fils, 1932–), vol. 3, col. 1222–91.

11. Augustine, *De magistro,* nn. 36–46 (XII–XIV); Bonaventure, *Christus unus omnium magister,* esp. nn. 20–28.

12. See n. 9.

13. I use here the Greek word "philosophia" to indicate a quest for wisdom in the line of philosophers from Plato to Proclus and theologians from Justin to deep in the Middle Ages. See "Philosophie" in *Historisches Wörterbuch der Philosophie* (Darmstadt: Wissenschaftliche Buchgesellschaft,1971–), vol. 1, col. 574–83, 592–99, 616–23, 630–33; Paul Rabbow, *Seelenführung: Methodik der Exerzitien in der Antike* (München: Kösel-Verlag, 1954); Pierre Hadot, *Exercises spirituels et philosophie antique,* 2d. ed. (Paris: Etudes Augustiniennes, 1987); Jean Leclerq, *Etudes sur le vocabulaire monastique du moyen âge* (Rome: Herder, 1961).

14. Bonaventure, *Comm. in Sent.,* III, dist. 23, art. 1, qu. 1: "Faith is nothing other than the habit through which our intellect voluntarily is caught in obedience to Christ" (cf. 2 Cor 10:5).

15. Dt 6:5 and Mt 22:37: "You shall love the Lord your God with all your heart, and with all your soul, and with all your mind."

16. See n. 14 and *Comm. in Sent.* III, dist. 23, art. 1, qu. 2, obj. 5 and corpus: "Fides habitus est per quem intellectus captivatur in obsequium Christi et innititur primae Veritati propter se."

17. 1 Cor 7:29–31.

18. 1 Cor 1:20–31; Eph. 3:14–19.

19. 1 Cor 7:31.

X. Theology Between Science and Spiritualiity

1. See chap. 7, n. 4.
2. 1 Cor 1:19–21; 2:4–5; 3:18–19; 4:7; Col 2:8.
3. Cf. chap. 5, n. 6.
4. Cf. Ruusbroec's descriptions of transcendence beyond essence, reason, and all manners or modes, e.g., in his summary of the contemplative adventure, *The Sparkling Stone* , in John Ruusbroec, *The Spiritual Espousals and Other Works,* intro. and trans. James A. Wiseman (New York: Paulist Press, 1985), pp. 153–84, esp. pp. 171–77.